Artfully Teaching the Science of Reading

This inviting book is a bridge between two major strands of reading instruction that are often held in opposition: the science of reading and artful approaches to teaching reading. Although the current climate of literacy instruction positions these approaches as diametrically opposed, the authors Young, Paige, and Rasinski describe how teachers can use the science of reading to engage students in artful, engaging, and authentic instruction. The authors reveal how effective teaching is a dynamic process that requires agency and creativity and show how teachers make artful shifts based on the needs of students in specific contexts. Chapters include a range of examples and explanations of how artful teaching is integrated into reading instruction and how it can increase students' motivation and positive attitudes toward reading. The concise and practical chapters cover key topics, including phonemic awareness, reading fluency, vocabulary, assessment, home and family reading, and more.

This essential road map for all pre-service and in-service reading teachers restores the importance of teacher agency, supports the critical understanding of reading research, and allows teachers to use their knowledge, experience, and creative approaches in the classroom. This is the definitive guide to teaching reading as both an art and a science.

Chase Young is Professor in the School of Teaching and Learning at Sam Houston State University, USA. He is editor of *Literacy Research and Instruction* and founding editor of *Journal of Teacher Action Research*.

David Paige is Professor of Literacy at Northern Illinois University, USA, and Director of the Jerry L. Johns Literacy Clinic. He is past president of the Association of Literacy Researchers and Educators.

Timothy V. Rasinski is Professor of Literacy Education and former director of the award-winning Reading and Writing Development Center at Kent State University, USA. He is past president of the Association of Literacy Educators and Researchers and is an elected member in the International Reading Hall of Fame. In a recent Stanford University study, Rasinski was identified as among the top two percent of scientists in the world.

Artfully Teaching the Science of Reading

Chase Young, David Paige,
and Timothy V. Rasinski

Routledge
Taylor & Francis Group

NEW YORK AND LONDON

Cover image: Getty images

First published 2022
by Routledge
605 Third Avenue, New York, NY 10158

and by Routledge
4 Park Square, Milton Park, Abingdon, Oxon, OX14 4RN

Routledge is an imprint of the Taylor & Francis Group, an informa business

Library of Congress Cataloging-in-Publication Data
Names: Young, Chase, author. | Paige, David (David D.), author. | Rasinski, Timothy V, author.
Title: Artfully teaching the science of reading / Chase Young, David Paige, and Timothy V Rasinski.
Description: New York, NY : Routledge, 2022. | Includes bibliographical references and index.
Identifiers: LCCN 2021054723 (print) | LCCN 2021054724 (ebook) | ISBN 9781032111469 (hardback) | ISBN 9781032080864 (paperback) | ISBN 9781003218609 (ebook)
Subjects: LCSH: Reading. | Reading, Psychology of. | Reading comprehension. | Books and reading.
Classification: LCC LB1050 .Y684 2022 (print) | LCC LB1050 (ebook) | DDC 418/.4071—dc23/eng/20211213
LC record available at https://lccn.loc.gov/2021054723
LC ebook record available at https://lccn.loc.gov/2021054724

ISBN: 978-1-032-11146-9 (hbk)
ISBN: 978-1-032-08086-4 (pbk)
ISBN: 978-1-003-21860-9 (ebk)

DOI: 10.4324/9781003218609

Typeset in Optima
by Apex CoVantage, LLC

Contents

Teaching Reading
A Science, but Also an Art

"I learned from my college courses in reading that fluency was a critical need for developing readers," says second grade teacher Sheely Kincaid, "and one of the best ways to improve fluency was to have students do what was called repeated reading or read one text several times. However, the way it was explained in class was that the purpose for the repeat readings was to have students read faster every time. That seemed kind of off for me. I'm trying to turn students into good readers, not necessarily fast readers." So Sheely decided to take a different approach to repeated readings. Every Monday, she would assign a new poem to pairs of students. "Then, throughout the week, we would 'rehearse' our poems – I would model the reading, read with students, and give them feedback and encouragement. We only spent maybe 10 to 15 minutes per day practicing our poems." Then, every Friday, students would perform their poems for classmates and other guests.

> It was a great way to end the week. Students felt like stars and had a natural motivation to rehearse their assigned texts. And, the rehearsal wasn't focused on reading fast, but reading with good expression that helps to convey the meaning of the poem. Here's the best part: I can't believe how students have improved. By midyear, every one of my students had met the winter benchmark for oral reading fluency (words correct per minute). Not once did I ask my students to practice reading fast!

Sheely's story is a great example of what we mean by scientific and artful teaching of reading. Reading fluency has been validated by scientific

DOI: 10.4324/9781003218609-1

research to be a critical competency for success in reading, and repeated reading has been found to be, again through scientific research, a viable and effective approach to improving fluency (and, in doing so, also improving overall reading proficiency). But rather than employ the common and somewhat artificial goal of increasing reading speed (as reading speed is one of several fluency measures), Sheely chose to consider a more authentic form of repeated reading – rehearsal in anticipation of a performance. Her results have been quite positive – students improve in the scientific measures of fluency, but also demonstrate a good deal of motivation and joy in reading for authentic purposes.

Let's face it: student achievement in reading has been relatively stalled for the past three decades. The National Assessment of Educational Progress (NAEP) has reported that reading achievement has been flat for over 30 years for both fourth grade and eighth grade students, the two grade levels assessed, in the United States. Moreover, the same NAEP report indicates that a substantial number of fourth and eighth graders read at a level considered below "proficient." This is not only a crisis in literacy development, but also threatens student learning and achievement in the disciplinary or content areas. Since much learning occurs through reading in the disciplinary areas, lack of proficiency in reading will logically limit student learning in those areas as well.

In response to this stagnation in reading achievement, there has been a growing recognition and embracement of science in understanding reading and the teaching of reading. In 2000, the National Reading Panel, a group of literacy scientists, conducted a comprehensive review of research on reading and reading instruction. The panel identified key competencies in reading, supported by scientific research, that should be taught for students to achieve proficiency in reading. These competencies, which most literacy teachers know, are phonemic awareness, phonics or word decoding, vocabulary or word meaning, reading fluency, and comprehension.

President George W. Bush's Reading First initiative, a plan to boost reading achievement among elementary grade students, was largely based on the findings of the National Reading Panel. Schools that bought into Reading First agreed to make the five elements of the panel nonnegotiable elements of their reading curriculum in kindergarten through third grade. The hope of Reading First was for every child to be reading at grade level by the end of third grade. Unfortunately, the hopes of Reading First were not realized. After multiple years of implementation, Reading First schools were compared with non-Reading First schools. No significant difference in reading achievement was detected among schools.

Rather than suggesting a reevaluation of how reading is taught in schools, the lack of significant results for Reading First resulted in doubling down on the need for science to guide or dictate how reading should be taught. The more recent Common Core State Standards, for example, identified specific competencies and sub-competencies that should be taught and that students should master in order to achieve reading proficiency. For accountability, teachers were then required, in many cases, to identify the specific standards that were being addressed in their teaching plans.

Brain scan studies examined portions of the brain that were activated during reading and detected differences between proficient and less proficient readers, especially students identified as dyslexic. The results of these studies most often suggested and pointed to the critical need for direct and systematic instruction in phonemic awareness and phonics. Indeed, in a recent series of articles written for the general public, educational journalist Emily Hanford suggested that lack of direct and systematic instruction, particularly in phonics, is the chief reason why so many students struggle in reading.

Despite these efforts, reading achievement, particularly among elementary students, has barely budged over the past three decades. The question we ask that guides this book is "Why?"

The Problem with a Science-Only Approach

Our own observations have led us to see how reading instruction that is solely or primarily driven by science can lead to some odd, if unintentional, manifestations. Science-informed phonics instruction argues the need for students to analyze the orthographic (spelling) structure of words. This has resulted in some phonics curricula in which children spend an inordinate amount of time reading nonsense words that feature various orthographic forms in isolation. Where in real life do people read nonsense words in isolation? In another example, scientific research has discovered that reading speed (number of words read correctly in a text per minute) is a good measure of automatic word recognition (fluency) and is highly predictive of reading comprehension and overall reading achievement among elementary students. This finding has resulted in instructional practice in which students are encouraged to practice reading as fast as possible in order to achieve or exceed the scientifically identified norm for reading fluency at their grade level. It isn't often that we as adults purposely engage in speed reading.

Science has also informed the development of tests for assessing students' comprehension and reading achievement. In instances too many to count, this has translated into students being given direct instruction and practice on how to take such tests and specifically on strategies for answering test questions that follow test passages that make up these reading assessments. None of these activities, as well as many others, even approximate real, authentic reading that we might find in life outside the classroom. When this type of instruction begins to take over an ever-larger portion of the previous minutes assigned for classroom reading instruction, many elementary grade students develop a flawed or skewed sense of reading, do not see a real purpose for reading or find satisfaction from reading, and are likely to increasingly disengage in reading. Reading instruction needs to be more than science only.

Science Yes, but Also a Need for Art

We contend, through this book, that what is missing from a "science-only" approach to reading instruction is an equal emphasis on what we term "artfulness" in teaching reading. An artful and scientific approach to reading instruction not only focuses on the need for developing proficiency in the various scientifically identified reading competencies and high achievement in overall reading proficiency, but also aims to develop in students a positive attitude toward reading and an inclination toward lifelong engagement with reading. Even scientists who have studied reading note the importance of artfulness necessary for reading instruction. Science of reading scholar Mark Seidenberg acknowledged in a *New York Times* article (Goldstein, 2020) that "the science that you need to know (reading acquisition) is good. The science on how to teach (reading) effectively is not." The quote often attributed to Mark Twain captures the risk of approaches to reading instruction that are scientific but do not emphasize the art of instruction: "The man who doesn't read good books has no advantage over the man who can't read them."

Indeed, what good is it to learn to read if in the process one does not also develop a recognition of the importance and utility of reading in one's life?

Education policy expert Benjamin Riley notes that scientific insights should inform the practice of reading, but teachers should still have the space for making pedagogical decisions about how reading instruction actually occurs. It is in this space where teachers are permitted to be artful. The most effective teachers of reading are ones who embrace both a scientific and artful disposition toward their reading instruction. It is this dual disposition that makes the best reading instruction so challenging. If you want to be a truly effective teacher, you must be an artist as well as a scientist. This is not an easy task. Too great an emphasis of one over another will lead to instruction that is stilted and less effective. It is finding the balance between art and science that is the goal of this book.

What Is Artful Reading Instruction?

Simply saying that reading instruction needs to be artful as well as scientific may sound like an appropriate goal, but what does it actually mean? In *Reading Research Quarterly*, a premier reading research journal, Paige et al. (2021) define the art of teaching as "being embodied in the teacher's decision making that involves selection, differentiation and delivery of engaging and efficacious reading instruction" (p. 1–2). The art of teaching reading does not deny the importance of science but recognizes teacher agency – the critical notion that what teachers do beyond the scientifically informed instruction matters.

We propose three critical features that help to define artfulness in any instruction, particularly reading instruction. Artful instruction needs to be authentic, aesthetic, and creative (Figure 1.1).

By reading instruction being authentic we mean that it should reflect what occurs in real life beyond the walls of the classroom or school. Perhaps a good way of considering the notion of authenticity is to think of

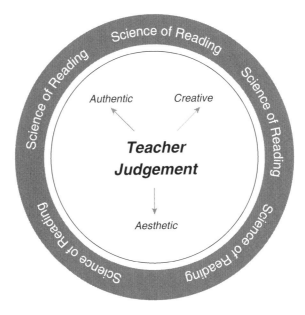

Figure 1.1 The model for artful instruction.

reading instruction activities and methods that may not be very authentic. Having students spend a significant amount of time reading nonsense words would not be considered very authentic. Similarly, engaging in daily timed readings in which students are encouraged to read fast is not something you are likely to encounter in real life. On the other hand, playing word games, engaging in deep discussions of texts, and reading a variety of text types are activities that you would experience in real life. Authenticity allows students to view and experience how the instruction they receive in school translates into real-life uses of literacy.

The word *aesthetic* is derived from the Greek word that means "feelings." Reading instruction that is aesthetic not only educates the mind, but also touches the heart. Years ago, Louis Rosenblatt wrote about reading that is efferent and reading that is aesthetic. The purpose of efferent reading is to understand and retain concepts, meanings, and facts presented in the text. In other words, efferent reading deals primarily with processing and accumulating information and knowledge. When you read a text (or have another experience in which information is intended to be conveyed) to learn about the events occurring in the world, or how to prepare a culinary dish, or how to repair your car, you are experiencing that text efferently.

In aesthetic reading, on the other hand, the focus for the reader is on the feelings, sensations, and emotions evoked during the reader's transaction with the text. When you read a text or have another experience that brings you to tears or sends a chill down your spine, you are having an aesthetic response to the reading or experience. If we as adults crave those aesthetic experiences in reading, shouldn't we allow and nurture children to have those experiences as well? We feel that all of us, children and adults, need to have experiences that are aesthetic as well as efferent.

Both types of reading, efferent and aesthetic, are important in and out of the classroom. However, it seems that there has been a decided privilege given to efferent reading. We can see this through the increasing emphasis on informational reading in our reading curricula. While we have no objection to efferent reading, when it comes at the expense of aesthetic reading experiences, such instruction becomes less artful. Scientific and artful reading instruction needs to be both aesthetic and efferent.

Art and Science Work Together

Art and science are not mutually exclusive endeavors. Many human activities are a blend of art and science. Although we often think of the medical field as being driven by science, there is clearly an affective or artful dimension to the practice of medicine. Indeed, we often use the term "medical arts" when referring to the practice of medicine. A medical doctor's bedside manner or the time that a doctor is willing to take with individual patients can affect the outcome of whatever medical treatment is prescribed.

It is science that often sets the parameters or boundaries within which art can operate. Take, for example, the visual arts. Early visual artists were limited by the technology that was available – colors, mediums, instruments, canvases, and so on. As science and technology advanced, so did art. New colors, new instruments, new media led to new styles and movements in the visual arts. Indeed, today, visual artists are exploring how art can be created, displayed, and distributed in digital environments.

Similarly, the musical arts were initially limited by science and technology. The earliest musical instruments were flutes and drums made from the animals and vegetation that was available. As musical science advanced, new instruments (such as stringed instruments and horns) became available and new ways of making, performing, and sharing music evolved. Over the last several decades, turntablism, the art of manipulating sounds and creating new music, sound effects, and other creative sounds and beats, typically by using two or more turntables, has emerged as a major form of music. Moreover, recording and sharing music with a wider audience has definitely benefitted from the scientific inventions of the phonograph and Internet.

The computer itself is usually viewed as a scientific and technology artifact. Yet, it took an artful approach to computers for them to become the ubiquitous part of human life in the twenty-first century. In a 2010 interview with Walter Isaacson, Apple computers cofounder Steve Jobs articulated his view of computers as being both scientific and artful:

> I always thought of myself as a humanities person, but I liked electronics. Then I read something that one of my heroes, Edwin Land of Polaroid, said about the importance of people who could stand at the intersection of humanities and sciences, and I decided that is what I wanted to do.

And, of course, it is clear the impact that Apple computers and products have had on the world.

When we claim that any human activity can only be defined and explored as only science or art, we are placing false limitations on that activity and how that activity can flourish and improve the human condition. Such is true for learning, and such is particularly true for learning to read. Certainly, science can tell us important aspects of reading and learning to read, and science can help us understand how the ability to read develops in humans. But is though art that teachers and students transform the possibilities of scientific theory and knowledge into human reality. This is the challenge facing all teachers, whether they work in a school or are parents doing their best at home to move children to higher levels of literacy and literacy achievement. And this is the challenge we wish to explore with you in this book – making science and art go hand in hand in growing proficient, strategic, and lifelong readers who employ this skill for the greatest personal and societal utility. Don't give up on science, but become that artist.

References

Goldstein, D. (2020, February 15). A New, Yet Old, Reading Exercise: Sound It Out. *New York Times*, Section A, p. 1.

Paige, D. D., Young, C., Rasinski, T. V., Rupley, W. H., Nichols, W. D., & Valerio, M. (2021). Teaching reading is more than a science: It's also an art. *Reading Research Quarterly*, 1–12. https://doi.org/10.1002/rrq.388

Becoming a Scientific and Artful Teacher

 Introduction

We define the art of teaching as being embodied in the teacher's decision-making that involves selection, differentiation, and delivery of engaging and efficacious reading instruction. We agree that instruction should be based on empirical research to ensure that we are developing the important aspects of reading. We know that children need instruction in phonemic awareness and phonics to crack the alphabetic code. Students also need effective reading fluency instruction to read accurately, automatically, and with appropriate expression. Vocabulary and comprehension instruction supports the main goal of reading – to understand and make meaning of text. An abundance of research exists that describes these important components and how they can be taught. As a reading teacher, you should familiarize yourself with these important components of reading instruction. In fact, you should be so familiar with them that they become second nature in your instruction, serving as a foundation for all that you do. However, how you teach reading and specific components can be up to you. This is where you are free to take the science of reading and arrange your instruction artfully.

You likely became a teacher for a lot of reasons, such as making a difference, impacting the world, and changing the lives of children, but you probably came in with some instructional ideas of your own. Sadly, it is possible that you might be told what and how to teach. Indeed, we are often told what to teach, and that can be helpful especially when it

DOI: 10.4324/9781003218609-2

is based on reading research. The scary part is when you are told how to teach. We come into education with our styles and ideas, and we should hold on to those. That is what makes us great teachers. Knowing how to count phonemes is important, but that is not what makes us great teachers. You are an effective teacher when you use your knowledge of reading instruction and add your own spin. The spin can be based on your own experiences and creativity, as well as your assessment of the students whom you serve.

The science of reading might have you thinking that you can teach anyone how to read as long as you go by the book. We regret to inform you that that is not how it works. There is more to it. Planning instruction before you know your students well will be hit or miss. As you develop relationships and learn their interests, learning styles, and abilities, you can tailor your instruction specifically for them.

Essentially, we need the teacher back in teaching. The science of teaching reading is simply the input into a creative teaching machine. The output is what students need. A few examples follow of creative, authentic, and aesthetic outputs. We have seen these in action and believe that they are good examples of teachers integrating the science and art of reading instruction. We hope that these examples serve to inspire you to weave your own instructional approaches.

Viviparous and Oviparous

We begin in a prekindergarten (pre-K) classroom where the teacher reinforces a science lesson about viviparous and oviparous animals with vocabulary instruction integrating Greek and Latin roots. Yes, you read that correctly – pre-K students learning Greek and Latin roots to help identify viviparous and oviparous animals. We can say with confidence that these kids were lucky to be in that classroom, as this teacher crafted a powerful lesson using science and art.

You are probably wishing you were in that classroom, too, as you are probably wondering what those terms mean. Are you smarter than a pre-kindergartner? Do not feel bad, as a four-year-old sitting next to me had to explain it. You will see how this is possible as we walk through a few aspects of the lesson.

The students were sitting in a circle on the floor, and the teacher first introduced two roots: *viv*, which means "alive" or "life," and *ovi*, which means "egg." She held up a stuffed puppy (which was super cute) and explained that this puppy is vivi, or "alive." She held up an egg and explained that it was known as ovi, which means "egg." She passed around the objects and asked each child to say the appropriate root as they held them. Hearing these very young children speaking Latin was awesome. The teacher engaged the students in a variety of multimodal ways to understand the roots, and certainly she had a wonderful rapport with these students. The exact strategies and the building of relationships was definitely part of the process, and you will learn with experience. At least at this point, you now have some idea of what viviparous and oviparous might mean.

The teacher introduced one more root – *parous*. Parous means "bearing" or "to produce." The students chanted it, talked about it, and defined it. The teacher pointed out that both terms, viviparous and oviparous, end with this root. We know the terms are related, but because of the vivi and ovi, we know they will have different meanings. In this context, the teacher explained that parous was referring to producing or having a baby. Fortunately, at this age, the conversation does not typically get too uncomfortable.

The teacher showed the students how to combine these roots. If we know that vivi means "life" and parous is "to produce a baby" (in this context), then we can put these meanings together to say that viviparous animals have live babies. Mind blowing, we know, and your brain is probably already constructing the meaning of "oviparous." We will give you a moment to think. Indeed, ovi means "egg," and therefore oviparous animals lay eggs. At this point, the teacher held up a series of photos of animals, both viviparous and oviparous, and encouraged the students to identify them – loudly. These little scientists were yelling at every picture and were accurate in their identifications.

Furthermore, these kids now had new insights into other words like vivid (lifelike) or revive (back to life). Scientifically speaking, we can also better understand the naming of species, such as the oviraptor, which means "egg thief," because scientists believed it stole eggs to survive (to live! See how that works?). Another type of raptor was quite fast, so they applied the *veloci* root, meaning "speed," and it was named the velociraptor. Now you, too, can impress your friends with your newfound scientific language (see Rasinski, Padak, Newton, & Newton, 2020).

We believe the theme of this story is: Aim high and go deep. If I was not sitting in that classroom, I would never have believed that four-year-old students could use their knowledge of Latin and Greek roots to better understand science concepts. This teacher, however, was unconstrained by these thoughts in her planning. She believed that her students should be treated as adept etymologists and scientists. She chose not to simply cover the material, but to make deep connections across the curriculum into important literacy concepts. She arranged some complex pieces into a comprehensible lesson comprised of science and art.

Generating Readers' Theater Scripts

Use of Readers' Theater in the classroom is a well-established activity to improve reading fluency and overall reading ability (see Young & Rasinski, 2009). Typically, teachers locate scripts online for the students to rehearse throughout the week and eventually perform for an audience. Indeed, this is already a blend of the science of repeated readings and the art of performance. However, this teacher took it a step further, integrating several more scientific concepts in literacy and even more in art.

Why not make life a little easier on you? Locating the perfect scripts for each week can get old. In this example, we describe how students write their own scripts and use them in their weekly routine. We have seen this approach with students as young as first grade, and it can easily be used into college. After students gain experience with Readers' Theater scripts, they can begin to write their own. At first, students can use mentor texts to write their scripts. Students choose one of their favorite texts of any genre and engage in the scripting process. Teaching this skill takes a lot of modeling, mentoring, and coaching, but eventually, students can produce scripts on their own (see Young & Rasinski, 2011). Moreover, once students are comfortable using mentor texts, they can begin to manipulate the text into parodies, a more complex process that requires an even deeper understanding of the text. We have seen students twist their favorite texts into some humorous adaptations, such as *The Pigeon Finds a Hot Dog!* (Willems, 2004) into *Sophia Finds a Turtle*. It was classic.

Thus far, the students have engaged in a meaningful and creative process of turning their favorite books into scripts. These scripts then become choices for the traditional Readers' Theater activity. Groups of students rehearse texts written by their peers and perform them for an audience. This is where the art really shines. The children who wrote the texts hear their scripts performed. They are authors. I interviewed some second graders after the process and asked, "How do you feel about being an author?" One young author responded, "I feel happy, and I feel like I'm going to be famous one day!" Amazing! We want our students to create something daily that is meaningful, authentic, and creative. She had such pride in her work that she truly believed it would bring her notoriety. We think all our students should go home each day wondering when their work that day will be world renowned.

Scientifically speaking, the students have read texts with a goal for deep understanding and an authentic purpose, both of which should lead to greater reading comprehension overall. The students also considered how the text could be modified into a script – a task that requires the knowledge of text structure and the author's intended meaning. Then, students are required to write, an important part of any literacy classroom. Students also revise and edit as necessary and produce a final script. These scripts are then rehearsed, which builds reading fluency, in that students need to read aloud with accuracy, at an appropriate pace, and with great expression. Artfully speaking, the teacher wove many important concepts into an authentic, creative, and aesthetic activity where students could improve their literacy skills in the context of something meaningful and authentic.

Student-Produced Movies

We now describe an artful approach to instruction that integrates several literacy experiences. Students create movies based on their reading. The art of creating movies based on texts requires students to reflect on their reading preferences, explore genres, engage in purposeful reading, compose summaries, visually represent a sequence of events, write scripts, and use technology. In addition to those important and research-based literacy processes, students engage in an authentic, creative, aesthetic, and fun activity (see Young & Rasinski, 2013).

The origin of this activity came from a teacher's desire to teach summary in a more authentic way. Finding ways to motivate students to write summaries had always eluded this teacher. We often hear of teachers introducing the concept of summary as simply a necessity in reading education with no real explanation of why students are writing summaries. We do not blame teachers for being honest and maybe stating, "We are learning summary because we have to. It is tested. It is boring, but it is necessary." However, this teacher looked to project-based learning and how summary might be integrated into something more – something bigger, something awesome. In the context of student-produced movies, you will see that the teacher artfully (if not sneakily) disguises summaries as a part of the script treatment – a real term used in the moving-making process. But first, we start from the beginning and briefly describe the steps.

Students are grouped based on their preferred genre of text, which requires them to reflect on what they like to read. Once groups are formed based on preferred genres, the students explore texts within that genre, perhaps thinking about some favorites read recently, or even considering texts they believe would make great movies. Upon deciding, student groups each create script treatments.

The script treatment begins with a summary of the text. The teacher tells the students that the summary is important so that the producer (the teacher) can evaluate whether the text is suitable for production. It must include the main idea and key points of the text so the producer has enough information about the text to make a decision: a go picture (yes, go forth and plan your movie) or a no picture (back to the drawing board). Naturally, students spend a great deal of time reading and rereading the text, making notes about important details – and constructing a good summary – because they want to make their movie. The script treatment also includes role assignments, including actors, director, camera operator, and so on. Although the original idea was based on a realization that summary could be taught in the context of something authentic, many processes were included as well.

The next step required students to visually represent sequences of events, or – as they call it in the movie business – storyboarding. The movie production team (or group) drew each scene to be filmed in order – yet another reading skill being taught in a creative and authentic way. These storyboards helped the director and the team organize each scene. At this point, students also began to transfer their text into a script suitable for a movie.

Once the storyboards and scripts were complete, production teams met with the teacher for a preproduction conference. In this conference, the teacher ensured that students could successfully make their movie. That involved making sure that the selected filming locations were reasonable and that the props could be obtained, and essentially mitigating any potential issues that might impede the groups' success. Approved groups then rehearsed until filming, which consequently also builds fluency. After the fun and sometimes chaotic filming process, the scenes were uploaded to computers and free software was used to edit the videos. Indeed, there were plenty of (hilarious) bloopers, so the teams had to decide on the best takes, order the takes, create transitions, and add music, titles, and credits. The students easily navigated the movie-making software and even taught the teacher about some neat features. The teacher held movie premieres after final production, and the kids were so excited. In fact, students years later still watch their not-so-major motion pictures. They can watch their masterpieces for eternity thanks to a teacher who weaved the science of reading and artful teaching into a project that was authentic, creative, and aesthetic.

Mystery Boxes

Another teacher used mystery boxes to build background knowledge and encourage discussion prior to reading a text. Prior to a read aloud, the teacher grouped the students and gave them each a box. In the box were items that represented aspects of the story that she was about to read. You could see intrigue and excitement on the students' faces the minute they opened the box. They immediately began taking the items out of the box, and the conversation began to roll. Students were making connections, inferring, drawing conclusions, summarizing possible stories, determining the main idea, making predictions, and having a great time. It seems like a long list of processes, but each of these were observed, and each happen to be named comprehension strategies by the National Reading Panel (National Institute of Child Health and Development, 2000) that are supposed to be effective for reading comprehension.

Too often, have we seen curriculum guides that separate reading comprehension strategies into different weeks. For example, in the first week, students learn to make connections and, in the next week, they learn to infer. The following week's focus is summarizing. Eventually, they get to main idea and a week later they make predictions. Simply because the research may only focus on one at a time does not mean we should teach them one at a time. In this example, mystery boxes, the teacher has not even instructed the students directly in all of the strategies; rather, the strategies were used organically and as necessary throughout the conversation in order to generate ideas about the text the teacher planned to read. As you can see, rather than in six weeks of instruction, students used at least six comprehension strategies in five minutes. Not only is that efficient, but the activity was authentic and engaging. The strategies emerged as a consequence of the activity. This teacher created a context that motivated students to critically think about text.

Essentially, this strategy engages learners, provides a purpose for reading and learning, and builds background knowledge before written text is even introduced. Furthermore, it is not an elaborate lesson that requires weeks of preparation and two weeks to complete. This teacher used what she knew about kids and their natural curiosity to prompt the use of reading comprehension strategies and critical thinking.

On the Fly

Up until now, we have described planned activities that integrated the science of reading with artful teaching. We also define artful teaching as dynamic, in that teachers can pivot when necessary to maximize the learning of their students. The ability to adjust teaching on the fly is certainly a skill of an artful teacher. You may need to be on page 349 of your basal reader by a particular date, but never skip a teachable moment to get there.

We saw a teacher use a district benchmark reading test as a lesson in the purpose for reading. Many of the students had completed the exam and were sitting quietly at their desks waiting for everyone to finish. No, they were not allowed to read or do anything else, because the district felt that it would cause students to rush through the text believing they could do something more interesting after it was done. Interesting caveat:

a study revealed that more time spent using test-taking strategies (such as looking back into the text, underlining, and reading the question first) was actually associated with lower scores (de Milliano, van Gelderen, & Sleegers, 2016). What? How can that be? Well, those students who could read proficiently simply read the text, understood it, and answered the questions correctly. This suggests that our focus should be on teaching kids how to read better – a suggestion with which we happen to agree.

Throughout the test, the teacher had noticed some frustration and also some bored faces. When all the students were done, the teacher instructed them: "Raise your hand if you think this test is important." All the students raised their hands – clearly a classroom full of teacher pleasers. Then, the teacher stated, "I don't think it is." Well, the students were shocked. The teacher asked again: "Do you think this test is important?" No one raised their hands. "Why not?" asked the teacher.

One of the students said that none of the passages were interesting. Indeed, that test was not important to him because he was not invested. Another student said, "It asked about some words and what they meant, and I could easily look them up if this was not a test." Interesting. This student was living in the real world where information is only a click away rather than in a "test world" – a world that does not actually exist. Another student mentioned that this test was only important for grades and that his mom might buy him ice cream if he did well. The conversation continued as they critically examined the test-taking genre and the purpose of reading.

The teacher had no idea where the conversation was going. That much was clear. However, something emerged. The students shifted their conversation from "Why are we even doing this test?" to "What are the real purposes of reading?" From that conversation, the classroom collective inductively came up with several authentic purposes for reading: 1) for fun, 2) to learn, and 3) to function in the real world. We are sure the teacher had at some point communicated purposes for reading, but in this case, the students discovered it for themselves. That which you discover, you own. In this instructional pivot, a standardized test was used to uncover and internalize an important concept about reading.

This next example of dynamic and artful teaching was based entirely on the needs of a student. In a practicum course at the university, a pre-service teacher was matched with a student to tutor weekly. The eight-year-old student was new to the class and, according to the teacher, was not doing well. So, the pre-service teacher worked with the professor to create an instructional plan for the student. Not long into the first session, the pre-service teacher realized that the student spoke very little English and seemed withdrawn. The professor spoke with the counselor and found out that the boy had just been released from a migrant detention center and was still separated from his family. The pre-service teacher and professor immediately dumped their plans, as it was not what the student needed. Instead, they gave him a tour of the school, put labels throughout, and redirected their focus to teaching him English so he would at least know what was happening around him. It was clear that this student would not benefit from being on page 349 in the basal reader.

Be "That Teacher"

As you read through the next chapters, be thinking about how our examples of artful teaching might inspire your own. We do not want you to follow our examples exactly. We want you to become an artful teacher who paves the way in reading instruction. We want you to be *that teacher* – the one who guides students to the edge of possibility, who uses challenge as motivation, and who learns beside their students. Be that teacher who provides meaningful and authentic experiences. Be that teacher who loves to teach. Be that teacher that students remember forever.

References

de Milliano, I., van Gelderen, A., & Sleegers, P. (2016). Types and sequences of self-regulated reading of low-achieving adolescents in relation to reading task achievement. *Journal of Research in Reading, 39,* 229–252. doi:10.1111/1467-9817.12037

National Institute of Child Health and Human Development. (2000). *Report of the national reading panel. Teaching children to read: An evidence-based assessment of the scientific research literature on reading and its implications for reading instruction (NIH publication no. 00–4769).* Washington, DC: U.S. Government Printing Office.

Rasinski, T., Padak, Newton, R., & Newton, E. (2020). *Greek and Latin roots: Keys to building vocabulary* (2nd ed.). Huntington Beach, CA: Shell Education.

Willems, M. (2004). *The pigeon finds a hotdog*. New York: Hyperion Books for Children.

Young C., & Rasinski, T. (2009). Implementing readers theatre as an approach to classroom fluency instruction. *Reading Teacher, 63*(1), 4–13.

Young, C., & Rasinski, T. (2011). Enhancing authors' voice through scripting. *Reading Teacher, 65*(1), 24–28.

Young, C., & Rasinski, T. (2013). Student produced movies as a medium for literacy development. *Reading Teacher, 66*(8), 670–675.

3 Artful Teaching of Phonemic Awareness

Nicole is in the spring of first grade. Her teacher, Ms. Thompson, has been teaching first grade since she entered the profession 11 years ago. Before attending Main Elementary, many of the children had spent considerable time engaged with books. Very often, they were read to by their parents well before they attended school. As a result of their early literacy exposure, many came to school with significant preliteracy skills; some even knew their alphabet letters while others could read a few words by sight.

Ms. Thompson has been teaching beginning and ending blends to her students for the last month. She noticed that in small-group instruction, Nicole was having difficulty reading consonant blends such as /cl/ and /st/ as in the words *clap* and *step*. When Ms. Thompson asked Nicole to blend the sounds in each of the words, Nicole tried to pronounce /cl/ as /c/ and would blend them as "/c/ – /a/ – /p/ . . . *cap*." When asked how many sounds are in /cl/, Nicole told Ms. Thompson that there was "one – the /c/ sound." Nicole gave a similar answer for /st/ in *step*. Nicole did not yet understand that consonant blends are composed of two sounds that are blended together. As Ms. Thompson thought about Nicole, she thought of several other students who were having similar problems with consonant blends, and she wondered why. She wondered if their challenges had anything to do with phonemic awareness.

DOI: 10.4324/9781003218609-3

Reading As Language

Zhurova (1963) and Elkonin (1963) were two Russian psychologists who were the first to report a relationship between phonemic awareness and learning to read. To artfully teach early reading, it is essential that the teacher has a basic understanding of the relationship between reading and language. Decoding written text is largely a language-based activity because it fundamentally involves converting the sounds within written words to speech (Moats, 2020). Phonology is an area of linguistics that studies the speech-to-sound patterns of a spoken language (Gillon, 2018). Phonological awareness is a broad, "umbrella" term that refers to the understanding that speech consists of units of language that decrease in size from the word to the syllable, to onset and rime, and finally to the phoneme level.

Phonological awareness is one of the five areas identified by the National Reading Panel (2000) as being critical to reading development (Ball & Blachman, 1991). Within the speech system of any language, a phoneme is the smallest unit of sound in the language. For example, in English, the word *frog* has four phonemes, /f/, /r/, /o/, and /g/, and these sounds can be blended together to pronounce *frog*. However, learning to speak does not require attention to individual phonemes; rather, one learns to pronounce blended phonemes as a whole word. Not every letter in a word represents a phoneme, and very often two or more letters represent a single phoneme. An example would be the four letters /eigh/ in the word n*eigh*bor that are combined to make the long /a/ sound.

Learning to hear individual phonemes within words is difficult for several reasons. First, in learning to speak, children hear a word as one, unitary sound. It is not necessary to focus attention to the phoneme level to acquire language. Second, when we speak, the phonemes inside words quickly overlap each other. In other words, they are coarticulated, which makes the recognition of individual phonemes difficult. Third, because we don't pay attention to the phonemes within words, recognizing their presence means attention must be explicitly directed to segmenting the word into its component parts. Indeed, it has been estimated that approximately 20 percent of children in the middle of first grade do not have sufficient phonemic awareness to profit from phonics instruction (International Reading Association, 1998). Developing phonemic awareness takes instruction and practice, and the artful teacher knows how to lead students in developing this skill (Blachman, 2000).

Phonological and Phonemic Awareness

Phonological and phonemic awareness are often confused, and it's easy to understand why. With that said, it's important that artful teachers have a clear sense of the difference. Phonological awareness is often called an umbrella term that means one has awareness of the various properties of the sounds within words. These properties include awareness of rhyme, alliteration (repetition of an initial consonant as in *picture perfect*), syllables, onsets, rimes, and phonemes within words. As you can see, phonological awareness is composed of several units within a word that decrease in size, resulting in a phoneme. However, because phonemic awareness is such an important part of phonological awareness, it is often discussed as its own entity. A phoneme is the smallest unit of sound within a word and English has 44 of them, some formed by a single letter and others composed of two or more. Phonemic awareness means that one can identify or isolate the phonemes (sounds) within a word. It also means the individual can manipulate phonemes as evidenced by the ability to delete a phoneme from a word and identity the new word or replace one phoneme with another to create a different word. Children possessing phonemic awareness are aware of the sounds within words and have acquired the ability to auditorily manipulate those sounds in spoken words (Goswami, 2000). A child who can hear and manipulate the sounds within a word could be asked to auditorily replace the /ĕ/ sound in *get* with the /ā/ sound and identify the new word as *gate*. Unlike speech development that occurs naturally through exposure to language, phonological and phonemic awareness requires intentional instruction to become aware of sounds at the syllable, onset-rime, and phoneme level. When walking through the halls of an elementary school, one might hear a teacher leading her students in an activity where they clap out the syllables in words – "to/geth/er, re/mem/ber, as/tro/naut/." This activity helps children tune their ear to the syllables within words. It also helps the child to eventually arrive at the insight that words are not one sound but are made up of smaller parts.

Nursery Rhyme Knowledge

Learning to identify words that rhyme is one of the earliest and easiest tasks that put children on the road to phonological awareness. Many of us were read nursery rhymes as very young children by our parents, caregivers, and older siblings. There are good reasons why an artful teacher would use nursery rhymes to build early reading skills in children, beyond the fact that they are so enjoyable.

To begin, researchers have found that preschool children who have knowledge of nursery rhymes are more likely to have future success in reading and writing (Bradley & Bryant, 1983, 1985; Vloedgraven & Verhoeven, 2007). Why might this be? To recognize words that rhyme requires children to identify similar sounding linguistic units within words. For example, *might*, *kite*, and *bright* all rhyme because of the long /i/ sound followed by the /t/ in each of the words. It is thought that instruction with rhymes teaches the child to focus attention on the abstract linguistic units within words, such as the long /i/ in our example (Treiman, 1985). Goswami (1986, 1988) points out that children who recognize rhymes later transfer this skill to reading word analogies such as *peak* and *beak*. Researchers have found that the relationship between nursery rhyme knowledge and phonological awareness is strong with long-lasting effects (Maclean, Bryant, & Bradley, 1987). In their study, Maclean and colleagues (1987) found that rhyming knowledge helped children become aware of word parts and possibly even letter sequences. This is an important development, as the ability to identify similar words by their parts is related to future reading skills (Goswami & Bryant, 1986). While nursery rhymes are often thought of as preschool material, they are effective for all primary-aged children (Samuels & Farstrup, 1992). Later in this chapter, we'll discuss artful strategies involving nursery rhymes.

 # Phonological Structure of Words

There is a general consensus among researchers that early reading success is dependent on acquiring phonemic awareness skills and that deficits in this area, along with letter knowledge and rapid automatized naming, account for differences in learning to read (Hulme, Bowyer-Crane, Carroll,

Duff, & Snowling, 2012; Caravolas et al., 2012; Hulme & Snowling, 2014; Melby-Lerväg, Lyster, & Hulme, 2012). Phonological awareness develops in stages beginning with a word as the basic unit of speech. Children then learn that words can be broken into smaller units called syllables. Through additional instruction, phonemic awareness continues to develop in stages as children become aware of the *initial* sound in a word, followed by the *final* sound, and lastly, children learn to identify the *medial* (middle) sound (Hulme & Snowling, 2009; Stahl & Murray, 1994).

To better understand this structure, Figure 3.1 provides a schematic that breaks down the phonology of words into four increasingly segmented levels that include the 1) word, 2) syllable, 3) onset and rime, and 4) phoneme levels. For example, you may know that a *gasket* is a round piece of rubber that fits inside the nozzle of a garden hose to keep it from leaking. While we recognize *gasket* as a single word, it has several layers of sounds. Remember that a syllable must contain a vowel sound, which means *gasket* can be broken down into two syllables. The first syllable is /găs/, as it contains a short /ă/ sound, while /kĕt/, the second syllable, has a short /ĕ/ sound. Also, the first syllable in *gasket* is stressed or accented, while the second syllable is unstressed. A stressed syllable such as /gas/ is pronounced with slightly more volume than is an unstressed syllable. Try

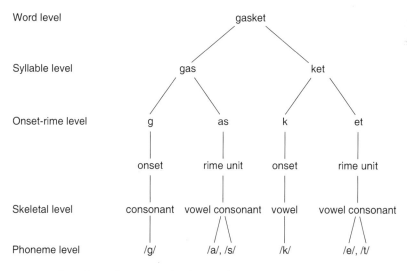

Figure 3.1 Phonological structure for the word *gasket*.

pronouncing *gasket* by putting the stress on the second syllable and you'll see it sounds quite different.

Each syllable can be further broken into its onset and rime. The onset is the initial (or beginning) consonant or consonant cluster in a word, while the rime is the vowel following the onset in the syllable. In the syllable /gas/, the onset is the /g/ sound, while /as/ is the rime, as it follows the initial sound. In the syllable /ket/, the onset is the /k/ sound, while /et/ is the rime. Finally, the onset and rime for each syllable can be reduced to their phonemes. The onsets in both /gas/ and /ket/ are the phonemes /g/ and /k/. The rime in both words has two phonemes each, /a/ and /s/ in *as*, and /e/ and /t/ in *et*.

The critical understanding here is that for students to be able to "unlock" a word from print to determine its pronunciation, they must be able to break down its sound structure. Understanding that a word can be reduced to syllables, parts within syllables, and then individual phonemes provides young readers with fundamental strategies to eventually decode words. Once learned, this process enables orthographic mapping, the scientific process by which the reader can easily convert letters to phonemes that "bonds spellings, pronunciations, and meanings of specific words in memory" (Ehri, 2014, p. 5). The orthographic mapping process is the mechanism that enables children to automatically read tens of thousands of words by sight and, through practice, become fluent readers. Understanding how phonological and phonemic awareness affects learning to read, and the instructional strategies needed for its development, is key to delivering the artful instruction needed by early readers.

For many children and even bright adults, a phoneme is a not-so-obvious, abstract concept that needs to be made explicit (Perfetti, Beck, Bell, & Hughes, 1987). Fortunately, considerable evidence exists that phonemic awareness can be taught and that it has significant, positive effects on learning to read (Blachman, Ball, Black, & Tangel, 1994; Lundberg, Frost, & Petersen, 1988). Once the door to phonemic awareness has been opened through instruction, it continues to develop as a result of learning to read (Bishop, 2003; O'Connor & Jenkins, 1999). In the next section, we will discuss several of the important strategies that facilitate the acquisition of phonemic awareness in children.

Stops and Continuous Sounds

Phonemes can be sorted into two categories: those that have an abrupt ending or stop and those that have a continuous ending that can be voiced without disruption for several seconds. Stop sounds include /b/, /d/, /q/, /h/, /j/, /k/, /p/, and /t/, while continuous sounds are made by /f/, /l/, /m/, /n/, /r/, /s/, /v/, /w/, /y/, /z/, /a/, /e/, /i/, /o/, and /u/. A common error when teaching stop sounds is when /uh/, /tuh/, or /kuh/ is added after the phoneme making the stop sound. For example, the phoneme for /b/ is a small puff of air made by the lips, as in *boy*. Oftentimes, teachers may add /uh/ after /b/ to get /buh/, which is incorrect. Try pronouncing the one-syllable word *boy* as *buhoy* and you get a two-syllable word that would be confusing to a young student learning the phonetic structure of words. This makes it important that teachers learn the correct pronunciation of all the phonemes. An excellent video from the Rollins Center for Language and Literacy demonstrating correct pronunciation of the 44 phonemes can be found here: www.facebook.com/watch/?v=611008882574074

 ## Phonemic Awareness and Alphabet Knowledge

Growth in a child's phonemic awareness has been shown to be facilitated by orthographic knowledge – that is, the connecting of sounds with letters (Bradley & Bryant, 1983; Burgess & Lonigan, 1998). Helping children connect sounds with letters creates a reciprocal relationship between the two that begins with alphabet knowledge (Ehri, 2014; Morris, Bloodgood, Lomax, & Perney, 2003; Stahl & Murray, 1994). With the acquisition of alphabet knowledge, the child begins to identify the initial and ending consonant sounds in words, becomes able to read pre-primer words, and is able to spell simple words using their beginning and ending sounds (Barron, 1991; Lonigan, Burgess, & Anthony, 2000; Morris et al., 2003). Alphabet knowledge is critical to phonological awareness acquisition. For example, from a total of 113 beginning readers who knew at least 45 letters of the alphabet, Stahl and Murray (1994) found just one child who could not split an onset from its rime. Phonemic awareness and subsequent reading acquisition is also facilitated with letter and letter-feature instruction. However, before introducing letters, students should be able to aurally (by ear) segment and blend consonant-vowel-consonant (CVC) words (Carnine, Silbert, Kame'enui, & Tarver, 2010; Honig, Diamond, & Gutlohn, 2018). The reason for this is that simultaneously learning letter sounds and segmenting and blending can be confusing to children (Stahl, 1992). Once students have aurally mastered these skills with CVC words, the inclusion of letters can accelerate reading progress (Snow, Burns, & Griffin, 1998).

Artful Teaching of Phonological and Phonemic Awareness

Teaching Fundamentals

Foorman and Torgesen (2001) state that phonological and phonemic awareness instruction must be explicit; in other words, it requires that children be given clear explanations that do not assume they will *get it*. It also requires clear modeling by the teacher with examples and lots of time for practice. Other teaching fundamentals to remember are the following:

1. Phonological and phonemic awareness develops across a continuum from easier to more difficult tasks, which means that instruction must be systematic.

2. As shown in Figure 3.1, students first recognize the full word, followed by the idea of syllables within words, onset and rime within syllables, and finally, phonemes. Instruction should proceed in this same sequence.

3. Children are able to isolate or recognize the initial (first) sound in a word before they hear the final (ending) and medial (middle) sounds.

4. The fewer the phonemes in a word, the easier it is for children to blend or segment them.

5. Words containing continuous sounds are easier to blend than are those with stop sounds in the final position. An example is the

word *can* versus the word *cap*. The /n/ makes a continuous sound, while the /p/ in *cap* is a stop sound.

6. Some activities are done in a whole-class format; however, some students will mimic the responses of classmates without engaging in the necessary cognitive activity to learn a task. Phonemic awareness instruction is more effective in small groups where the teacher can more easily attend to individual children and their needs.

7. Phonemic awareness lessons should target just one or two skills at a time.

8. To help students move the abstract idea of sounds to a more concrete conceptualization, physical markers such as chips, buttons, or bottle caps are very helpful to represent abstract phonemes.

9. To avoid confusion, it is important for the teacher to correctly pronounce phonemes.

10. Instruction in phonological and phonemic awareness should be delivered in short sessions (5 to 15 minutes) with total instruction taking about 20 hours over the school year. However, not all children acquire phonology skills at the same rate and some may need additional time.

11. It is critical that students regularly be assessed as they develop phonemic awareness to ensure that they are acquiring the necessary skills.

12. Match phonological awareness instruction to the learner's level of orthographic knowledge, moving from easier to harder tasks.

Finally, remember that teaching phonemic awareness is simply a means to an end, as it helps children become better readers. When children can hear the phonemes within words, it makes it easier to connect them to letters. This skill increases the effectiveness of phonics instruction. Phonemic awareness also helps children better learn how to segment and blend the sounds within words, which also helps with correctly spelling words.

Artful Strategies

Identifying Words

Remember that the term "phonological awareness" refers to decreasingly smaller units of sound within words. Beginning at the word level, these sounds reduce to the syllable, onset and rime, and finally phoneme levels. Before proceeding to smaller units of sound, the artful teacher must first be certain that students understand the concept of a word. A simple way of helping students become aware of words is to aurally pronounce a sentence and have them use their finger to tap out the words on their desktop. Here's an example:

Practice Sentence: I Have a Dog

Teacher: Say to students: "Let's practice identifying words in a sentence by using our finger to tap out the individual words on our desk. For example, I'm going to tap out the words to the sentence *I have a dog*. Now watch what I do." At this point, the teacher is using a hard surface where all students can see her hand. "Watch my finger as I say the sentence aloud. For every word I say, I will tap my finger one time on the desktop. *I* (tap once) *have* (tap once) *a* (tap once) *dog* (tap once). How many times did I tap my finger?"

Students: "Four times."

Teacher: "That's right. I tapped my finger four times. So how many words are in the sentence?"

Students: "Four."

Teacher: "That's correct. Now let's try two more sentences."

At this point, the teacher uses two more sentences to be sure that all students have the idea:

It rained all day (four words).

I took my dog to the park (seven words).

We suggest that at this early stage, it is better to use single-syllable words, as multisyllabic words may confuse students. Have students practice several more sentences with an elbow partner to reinforce learning. It would be best to revisit this activity over several days and formatively assess each child to be certain they have mastered the skill before moving on to identifying syllables.

Syllabication

Once all students have mastered the concept of a word, it's time to move to identifying syllables within words. One way to begin is to have students blend two single-syllable words into one. For example:

Teacher: "Let's take two small words and put them together to make one, bigger word. Let's use the words *bird* and *house*. Can you put the words *bird* and *house* together to make one word? Tell your elbow partner what that word is."

Students: Students turn to their partners and say, "Birdhouse."

Teacher: "When we combine *bird* and *house* to make one word, we get *birdhouse*, don't we? Now let's try two more pairs of words that we can combine to make bigger words. What big word do *high* and *way* make?"

Students: "Highway."

Teacher: "What big word do *air* and *plane* make?"

Students: "Airplane."

Teacher: "I think you're getting the idea!"

Syllable Segmentation

Distribute additional practice opportunities over several days so that students firmly understand how words can be combined to make a single word. Once students understand that two words can be combined to make a bigger word, it's time to help them break one word into two smaller words. A way to help students divide words is to clap them out. Here's an example:

Teacher: "Can we combine the words *some* and *thing* into one word? Yes, we can. What word would that be?"

Students: "Something."

Teacher: "That's correct. The new word is *something*. Now I can break the word apart by clapping. Watch and listen: *some – thing*." (Clap once while simultaneously saying *some* and again on *thing*.) "Now watch and listen as I clap out another word: *to – day*. Now everyone clap and say *today* with me: *to – day*."

Have students practice with several words that's followed by practice with additional, different words over the next several days. Once students have the idea that they can clap apart two one-syllable words, it's time to transition to clapping out multisyllabic words that are other than compound words. Before we move on, let's review the scaffolded, artful approach we've used so far.

1. First, we helped students learn the concept of a word by tapping out the words within sentences.

2. Next, students took two single-syllable words and combined them into a "big" word, in essence making a compound word.

3. We then taught students to "split" single-syllable compound words by clapping.

4. As a next step in this artful sequence, we used clapping to transition students to focus on syllables within words.

Teacher: "Many words are made up of parts called syllables. The great thing about syllables is that we can clap them out just like we do when we split a big word into parts."

Teacher: "Now that you know how to clap out a big word into two smaller words, let's learn to clap out words with syllables. I'm going to clap out the syllables in the word *tomorrow*. Listen and watch as I do it: *to – mor – row*." How many times did I clap?"

Students: "Three times."

Teacher: "That's because there are three syllables, or parts, in the word *tomorrow*. Listen and watch as I clap out the syllables in the word *tangerine*: *tan – ge – rine*. How many syllables are in *tangerine*?"

Students: "Three."

Teacher: "That's right. There are three syllables in *tangerine*. Now I want you to clap out syllables with me. Let's clap out the syllables in the word *tomorrow*. Are you ready? I'll count down, 3–2–1, and then we'll begin. Ready? Three, two, one: *to – mor – row*. How many syllables are in *tomorrow*?"

Students: "Three."

Teacher: "Very good. Now let's clap out the syllables in *tangerine*. Three, two, one: *tan – ge – rine*. That's right."

Practice should continue and be distributed over several days using a bank of three- and four-syllable words. Students should be individually assessed using four or five words that were not included in the practice sets to be certain they have mastered the blending and segmenting of syllables.

Syllable Deletion

The final step in syllable awareness development is the ability to identify a word after a syllable has been removed. Let's say I remove the /er/ sound from the word *walker*. What word remains? The answer of course is *walk*. We can help children further hone their awareness of sounds within words by providing a series of practice words where they delete a syllable to make a new word. Here are some examples of such words:

Word/syllables/deletion/ remaining word	Word/syllables/deletion/ remaining word	Word/syllables/deletion/ remaining word
Gummy/gum-my/ my/**gum**	Cowardly/cow-ard-ly/ard-ly/**cow**	Nevermore/ne-ver-more/ ne-ver/**more**
Candy/can-dy/dy/**can**	Underline/un-der-line/der-line/**under**	Woolen/wool-en/en/**wool**
Mattress/mat-tress/ tress/**mat**	Helmet/hel-met/hel/**met**	Loveliest/love-li-est/ est/**lovely**

Nursery Rhymes

We all know the nursery song *Twinkle, Twinkle, Little Star*, as it was likely sung to us when we were infants, or we've sung or heard it sung to others. When we read or sing nursery rhymes to young children, we tend to use expression and animation that engages and delights the child. Children react to our emotion with outward signs such as smiles and laughs. In a very real way, we are teaching the child the power of interpersonal communication. And whether they understand the words or not, the child is hearing the richness of words, how they are connected to each other, and the importance of the cadence and rhythm of speech (prosody). Consider the 32 words of *Twinkle, Twinkle*. The child is hearing sentences repeated that reinforce the learning of new words and syntax. Children begin development of phonological awareness as they hear the emphasis on the initial sounds in words, such as the /t/ in *twinkle* and the /s/ in *star*. They are hearing the expression in our voice that communicates meaning and they are learning the tempo of speech and how it's connected to emphasis. For example, in the second sentence of the last stanza, we typically lower our voice on the final *are* to signal that the song is finished. Finally, the child is exposed to words that sound similar because they rhyme, as in *star/ are* and *high/sky*. In sum, teaching nursery rhymes delights and benefits children. By the way, the version of *Twinkle, Twinkle, Little Star* by the late Hawaiian singer Israel "Iz" Kamakawiwo'ole is one of the most beautiful ever recorded (www.youtube.com/watch?v=hNzG5G1BCUE).

> *Twinkle, twinkle little star,*
> *How I wonder what you are!*
> *Up above the world so high,*
> *Like a diamond in the sky.*
> *Twinkle, twinkle little star,*
> *How I wonder what you are!*

Let's discuss how to use nursery rhymes to teach phonological and phonemic awareness skills for 1) rhyming and 2) oddity tasks.

Rhyming

Help children learn that words can sound similar because they can share the same sound. Here's an example:

Teacher: "Listen to these two words: *bear* and *scare*. Do they sound similar? Listen to the sound near the end of the words: *b-ear* and *sc-are*. I hear *air* in both words. I'm going to stretch out the words so you can better hear *air*: *b-airrrrrrrrr* and now *sc-airrrrrrrr*. Do you hear the same sound in both words?"

Once children can hear the similarity, teach them the name for words that sound similar.

Teacher: "When words sound very similar, we say the words rhyme. Can you say *rhyme*? While the beginning of *bear* and *scare* sound different, the second part of the words sounds the same – and that's what makes them rhyme."

Introduce several other pairs of words to help reinforce the notion of rhyming words. Using a distributed practice approach over the next several weeks, frequently revisit rhyming words to reinforce the concept in your students.

Oddity Tasks

An oddity task is an activity where children identify what does not belong. Oddity tasks can help students hone their rhyming skills. For example, consider the poem *Itsy Bitsy Spider*:

The itsy bitsy spider climbed up the water spout.
Down came the rain and washed the spider out.
Out came the sun and dried up all the rain.
And the itsy bitsy spider climbed up the spout again.

We can select words from the poem to create an oddity task where students identify which of the three words sounds different from the other two. Let's consider the following three words:

spout, out, itsy

While *spout* and *out* share the same sound (out), *itsy* does not. This makes *itsy* the odd word that does not belong. Other word combinations can be created using words from the poem, such as:

came, rain, sun
itsy, dried, bitsy

Like many activities designed to build skills, using a distributive practice approach helps students build the strong cognitive connections that lead to mastery learning. Artful teachers learn to distribute practice sessions over several days and weeks to reinforce and solidify learning.

Developing Phonemic Awareness

Turtle Talk

We learned earlier that phonemic awareness is the ability to hear and manipulate phonemes, the smallest unit of speech in a language. "Turtle talk" is a method to help children learn to hear all the phonemes in a word (https://palsresource.info/wp-content/uploads/2020/05/PALS-Activities-for-Families-Turtle-Talk.pdf).

If you've ever watched a turtle walk, you know they proceed very slowly, which makes the idea of turtle "races" a bit of an oxymoron. The idea with turtle talk is to *slooooow* down the pronunciation of words so that all the phonemes in the word can heard. Often, in our normal adult speech, we talk so quickly that it can be difficult for young children to discriminate individual words and even sounds from one another. Turtle talk helps students tune their ears to the sounds within words and put them on the way to eventual phonemic awareness.

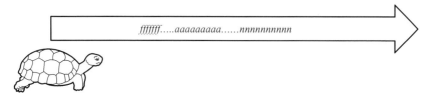

Figure 3.2 Move your turtle along each letter as you use turtle talk to pronounce each phoneme – *fffffffaaaaaaaannnnnnnnn*. Now have students take their arrowhead and turtle to pronounce *fan* with you. It may be necessary to have students practice with you several times to help them practice the motor skill of moving their turtle along the line.

To implement turtle talk, cut out a paper turtle and an arrowhead line for each of your students. If you prefer, a popsicle stick can be glued to each turtle as a handle.

Introduce the activity by telling students that they will participate in "turtle time." Ask students if they have ever watched a turtle walk. Have they noticed that they walk very slowly? Tell students that during turtle time, they will work on pronouncing words very slowly to mimic the way turtles walk.

Select several CVC words – for example, let's choose the word *fan*. Using an overhead or document camera, demonstrate to students how to stretch out the word *fan* using turtle talk. Be sure students can see you moving your turtle as you pronounce each phoneme.

Once students have gotten the idea, distribute practice over several sessions using one or two dozen words. When selecting words, be aware whether the letters in the CVC words are a stop or continuous sound. While continuous sounds can be elongated, a stop cannot. Take the word *bit*, for example – the letters /b/ and /t/ are stops, while /i/ is a continuous sound. Sounding out the word using turtle talk would look like this: *b . . . iiiiiiiiiiii . . . t*.

Another way to implement turtle talk is what we call "step-by-step" – turtle steps, that is. Model for students how to say a word as if their turtle were taking very slow steps. Let's turtle step the word *sat*:

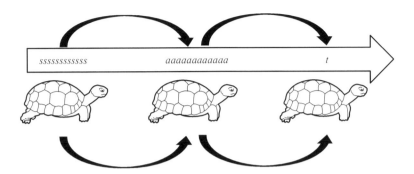

Figure 3.3 As you say each phoneme, move your turtle along *ssssssss* to *aaaaaaaaaa* to *t*.

Elkonin Boxes

Another tool to help students acquire phonemic awareness is an Elkonin box. Daniil Elkonin was a Russian psychologist who linked phonemic awareness to reading and developed the idea of boxes in the 1960s as a concrete way to help students identify phonemes. Elkonin boxes are simply squares on a piece of paper that help a student identify phonemes in a word by moving a token into a box for each phoneme they hear in a word. The use of a token takes the abstraction of a phoneme and makes it a bit more concrete for the student. Before using a Elkonin box, students will need some prerequisite skills. For example, they should be able to recognize syllables within words and identify their initial sounds. Elkonin boxes can be introduced as a whole-class activity, as they can help all students discover and practice identifying sounds at the initial, medial, and final positions.

In the graphic below, we've created an Elkonin box with four boxes. Boxes can be created on paper or drawn on a whiteboard with a dry-erase marker. The student should be provided with tokens of some kind that they can physically push into the Elkonin boxes. In the first example, we use the word *to*. If introducing Elkonin boxes for the first time, you will need to model the activity for the students. The lesson sequence would go as follows:

1. Tell the students that they are going to learn how to identify the sounds within words using something called an Elkonin box.

2. Explain to students that an Elkonin box is simply squares drawn on a page. Show them your Elkonin box on the overhead or at the table if you're with a small group. Explain to students what the tokens are and that they will each represent one sound in a word.

3. Tell the students that they will push one token into a box for each sound they hear in the word *to*.

4. Model for the students how to slowly pronounce the word, emphasizing each phoneme – as in *t-oooooooo* – by stretching out (also called rubber banding) the /o/ sound for emphasis.

5. Ask the students: "What is the first sound you hear in *to*?"

6. Students respond, identifying the /t/ sound.

7. Demonstrate how the token moves by pushing it into the first box. Be sure the students understand that the token represents the /t/ sound in the word *to*.

8. Now ask the students to identify the next sound they hear in the word *to*. It may be helpful to lead students again in stretching out the word so that all students hear the two sounds.

9. Students should respond that the second sound is /oo/.

Target wird: to

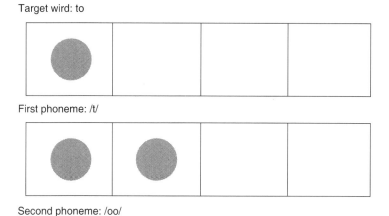

First phoneme: /t/

Second phoneme: /oo/

Figure 3.4 Now give the students a second word for them to analyze with you. Let's try a three-phoneme word – *sheep*. It would be helpful to show the students a picture of a sheep.

10. Now push the second token into the box immediately to the right of the first token.

11. Again, explain to the students that the first token represents the /t/ sound, while the second represents the /oo/ sound.

12. Ask the students if they hear any more sounds in the word to confirm that they have identified all the sounds.

1. Tell the students to remove the tokens from their Elkonin box.

2. Tell students that the next word will be *sheep*.

3. Lead the students in stretching out the word – *shhhhhh eeeeeeee p*.

4. Ask the students how many sounds they hear in the word. Confirm that they are hearing three sounds. Rubber band the word again if the students are having trouble hearing all three sounds.

5. Now ask the students to identify the first sound they hear.

6. Students should respond with the diagraph /sh/. As they identify the sound, they will move the token to the first box.

7. The second sound will be the long /e/ sound. After identifying the sound, students move the second token into the second box.

8. The third sound is the final consonant /p/. Students move the token into the third box.

9. Have the students review the three sounds and blend them together to pronounce *sheep*.

Students should now independently attempt to identify the phonemes within a word using an Elkonin box. Choose a two- or three-phoneme word and provide a picture. Allow students to work independently and then review the correct sound placements when everyone has had a chance to finish. Be aware of students who may be having difficulty. As students become comfortable with Elkonin boxes, words containing more phonemes can be used.

Phoneme Manipulation

Beyond phoneme isolation, students should also be able to delete and insert a new phoneme that results in a different word. While this is the most difficult of the phonological skills, mastery is critical to putting students on the road to reading success. To begin, let's consider an example where the first sound in a word is identified and then substituted with a new sound to make a new word:

Example 1:

Teacher: "Say tire."

Students: "Tire."

Teacher: "Now let's change *tire* to a new word. Instead of saying the /t/ in *tire*, say the /f/ sound. What word do we have now?"

Students: "Fire."

Example 2:

Teacher: "Say bit."

Students: "Bit."

Teacher: "Now instead of saying the /t/ sound at the end, what word do we have if we say the /g/ sound instead?"

Students: "Big."

Teacher: "Now say *big*."

Students: "Big."

Example 3:

Teacher: "Say *big*."

Students: "Big."

Teacher: "What word do we have if instead of saying the /i/ sound in *big*, we say the /u/ sound?"

Students: "Bug."

We discussed earlier that students learn to hear the initial sound in a word, then the last sound, and finally the medial sound. When implementing phoneme manipulation, we would have a number of words for students to practice initial phoneme manipulation before moving on to final and medial phonemes. Following this same developmental trajectory, we would have students practice with ending phonemes before challenging them with sounds in the medial location.

Another sequence can begin with a word to which a sound is added in the final position, and then replaced with another sound, as in the example below:

Teacher: "Now say *tire* without saying the /r/ sound."

Students: "Tie."

Teacher: "Now what word is *tie* if you add the /m/ sound at the end?"

Students: "Time."

Teacher: "Let's delete the /m/ sound and replace it with a /d/ sound. What word do we have now?"

Students: "Tide."

When students engage in a phoneme manipulation task, there are two ways they can arrive at an answer. If they know how to spell the word, they can project it in their mind's eye in working memory and manipulate the *letters* to arrive at the correct answer. It may well take several seconds to arrive at the correct answer this way. While the students may well arrive at the correct answer, they are no longer manipulating sounds. Rather, they are working with mental images of letters, which is no longer invoking phonemic awareness. For students fluent with the sounds in the word, they can perform the manipulation aurally and automatically without devoting any mental processing to the task and without the use of letters. This means they provide an answer within a second or even less. An automatic answer indicates that the student is fluent in manipulating *phonemes*.

This same process can be used with distributive practice over the course of several months. Remembering that children progress at different rates, some may take longer than others to acquire phoneme manipulation skill. Some other tips:

- Do not use words containing *x* and *qu*, as these contain two phonemes.
- Until students have mastered words with three phonemes, avoid longer words and those with blends.
- Words with r-controlled letter features and strong diphthongs such as /oy/ and /ou/ should be avoided until students know the sounds in isolation.

Sliding Caps

Another way to make phonemes less abstract is with the use of bottle caps or plastic chips of some kind. Each student has a pile of caps. A cap for each sound in a word is lined up on the student's desk. When there is a cap for each sound, students can sweep their finger below the caps to pronounce the word by blending the sounds together.

When substituting sounds, the student removes the cap from the word and replaces it with a new cap to signify the sound substitution. After the cap has been inserted, the student again uses a finger sweep to signify blending of the sounds to pronounce the word. This is a tactile way to help students remember that individual sounds are blended together to say the new word. The addition, deletion, and new sound insertion forms a sound chain – *tire-tie-time-tide*. The chart below shows the steps to go from *tire* to *tide*.

Target Word	Sound Deletion	New Word	Sound Insertion	New word	Sound Deletion	Sound Insertion	New word
Tire	/r/	tie	/m/	time	/m/	/d/	tide

 # Conclusion

In this chapter, we've provided a discussion of phonological and phonemic awareness and why it's important to successful reading acquisition. We have briefly mentioned the importance of formatively assessing children as they acquire phonological and phonemic awareness. We want to emphasize here that it cannot be assumed that because a child participates in instruction that they have acquired sufficient phonemic awareness. Because it is critical for reading development, it is imperative that at a minimum, children be assessed to ensure that they have phonemic awareness at the CVC level. We have also presented several examples of playful and artful instruction that encourages phonemic awareness development. There are other successful strategies for phonemic awareness, but in the end, they must encourage the isolation, blending, and manipulation of phonemes to equip the child with the necessary phonemic awareness foundation to profit from phonics instruction.

References

Ball, E. W., & Blachman, B. A. (1991). Does phoneme awareness training in kindergarten make a difference in early word recognition and developmental spelling? *Reading Research Quarterly*, 26(1), 49–66. Retrieved from https://login.auth.lib.niu.edu/login?url=www.jstor.org/stable/747731

Barron, R. W. (1991). Proto-literacy, literacy, and the acquisition of phonological awareness. *Learning and Individual Differences*, 3(3), 243–255. https://doi.org/10.1016/1041-6080(91)90010 -X

Bishop, A. G. (2003). Prediction of first-grade reading achievement: A comparison of fall and winter kindergarten screenings. *Learning Disability Quarterly*, 26(3), 189–200. https://doi.org/10.2307%2F1593651

Blachman, B. A. (2000). Phonological awareness. In M. L. Kamil, P. B. Mosenthal, P. D. Pearson, & R. Barr (Eds.), *Handbook of reading research* (Vol. 3, pp. 483–502). Mahwah, NJ: Lawrence Erlbaum.

Blachman, B. A., Ball, E., Black, S., & Tangel, D. (1994). Kindergarten teachers develop phoneme awareness in low-income, inner-city classrooms: Does it make a difference? *Reading and Writing: An Interdisciplinary Journal*, 6, 1–17.

Bradley, L., & Bryant, P. E. (1983). Categorizing sounds and learning to read – a causal connection. *Nature*, 301(5899), 419–421. https://doi.org/10.1038/301419a0

Bradley, L., & Bryant, P. E. (1985). *Rhyme and reason in reading and spelling*. Anne Arbor: University of Michigan Press.

Burgess, S. R., & Lonigan, C. J. (1998). Bidirectional relations of phonological sensitivity and prereading abilities: Evidence from a preschool sample. *Journal of Experimental Child Psychology*, 70(2), 117–141. https://doi.org/10.1006/jecp.1998.2450

Caravolas, M., Lerva°g, A., Mousikou, P., Efrim, C., Litavsky´, M., Onochie-Quintanilla, E., et al. (2012). Common patterns of prediction of literacy development in different alphabetic orthographies. *Psychological Science*, 23, 678–686. https://doi.org/10.1177%2F0956797611434536

Carnine, D. W., Silbert, J., Kame'enui, E. J., & Tarver, S. G. (2010). *Direct instruction reading* (5th ed.). Boston: Merrill.

Ehri, L. C. (2014). Orthographic mapping in the acquisition of sight word reading, spelling memory, and vocabulary learning. *Scientific Studies of Reading, 18*(10), 5–21. https://doi.org/10.1080/10888438.2013.819356

Elkonin, D. B. (1963). The psychology of mastering the elements of reading. In B. Simon & J. Simon (Eds.), *Educational psychology in the U.S.S.R.* (pp. 165–179). London: Routledge & Kegan Paul.

Foorman, B. R., & Torgesen, J. K. (2001). Critical elements of classroom and small-group instruction promote reading success in all children. *Learning Disabilities Research & Practice, 16*(4), 203–212. https://doi.org/10.1111/0938-8982.00020

Gillon, G. T. (2018). *Phonological awareness: From research to practice* (2nd ed.). New York: Guilford.

Goswami, U. (1986). Children's use of analogy in learning to read: A developmental study. *Journal of Experimental Child Psychology, 42,* 73–83. https://doi.org/10.1016/0022-0965(86)90016-0

Goswami, U. (1988). Children's use of analogy in learning to spell. *British Journal of Developmental Psychology, 6,* 21–34. https://doi.org/10.1111/j.2044-835X.1988.tb01077.x

Goswami, U. (2000). Phonological and lexical processes. In M. L. Kamil, P. B. Mosenthal, P. D. Pearson, & R. Barr (Eds.), *Handbook of reading research* (Vol. 3, pp. 251–268). Mahwah, NJ: Lawrence Erlbaum.

Goswami, U., & Bryant, P. E. (1986, March). *Rhyme, analogy and children's reading.* Paper presented at the Conference on Early Reading Acquisition, Center for Cognitive Science, University of Texas, Austin.

Honig, B., Diamond, L., & Gutlohn, L. (2018). *Teaching reading sourcebook* (3rd ed.). Oakland, CA: Arena Press.

Hulme, C., Bowyer-Crane, C., Carroll, J. M., Duff, F. J., & Snowling, M. J. (2012). The causal role of phoneme awareness and letter-sound knowledge in learning to read: Combining intervention studies with mediation analyses. *Psychological Science, 23*(6), 572–577. doi:10.1177/0956797611143592

Hulme, C., & Snowling, M. J. (2009). *Developmental disorders of language, learning and cognition.* Chichester, England: Wiley-Blackwell.

Hulme, C., & Snowling, M. J. (2014). The interface between spoken and written language: Developmental disorders. *Philosophical Transactions* of the *Royal Society of London B: Biological Sciences, 369*(1634), 20120395. doi:10.1098/ rstb.2012.0395

International Reading Association. (1998). *Phonemic awareness and the teaching of reading.* Newark, DE: International Reading Association.

Lonigan, C. J., Burgess, S. R., & Anthony, J. L. (2000). Development of emergent literacy and early reading skills in preschool children: Evidence from a latent-variable longitudinal study. *Developmental Psychology, 36*(5), 596–613. https://doi.org/10.1037/0012-1649.36.5.596

Lundberg, I., Frost, J., & Petersen, O. (1988). Effects of an extensive program for stimulating phonological awareness in pre-school children. *Reading Research Quarterly, 15*(2), 203–227. Retrieved from www.jstor.org/stable/748042

MacLean, M., Bryant, P. E., & Bradley, L. (1987). Rhymes, nursery rhymes and reading in early childhood. *Merrill-Palmer Quarterly, 33,* 255–281.

Melby-Lervåg, M., Lyster, S.-A. H., & Hulme, C. (2012). Phonological skills and their role in learning to read: A meta-analytic review. *Psychological Bulletin, 138,* 322–352. doi:10.1037/a0026744

Moats, L. C. (2020). *Speech to print: Language essentials for teachers* (3rd ed.). Baltimore: Brookes.

Morris, D., Bloodgood, J. W., Lomax, R. G., & Perney, J. (2003). Developmental steps in learning to read: A longitudinal study in kindergarten and first grade. *Reading Research Quarterly, 38*(3), 302–328. https://doi.org/10.1598/RRQ.38.3.1

National Reading Panel. (2000). *Teaching children to read: An evidence-based assessment of the scientific research literature on reading and its implications for reading instruction. National institute of health pub. No. 00–4769.* Washington, DC: National Institute of Child Health and Human Development

Perfetti, C. A., Beck, I., Bell, L. C., & Hughes, C. (1987). Phonemic knowledge and learning to read are reciprocal: A longitudinal study of first grade children. *Merrill-Palmer Quarterly, 33*(3), 283–319.

O'Connor, R. E., & Jenkins, J. R. (1999). Prediction of reading disabilities in kindergarten and first grade. *Scientific Studies of Reading, 3*(2), 159–197. https://doi.org/10.1207/s1532799xssr0302_4

Samuels, S. J., & Farstrup, A. E. (Eds.). (1992). *What research has to say about reading instruction*. Newark, DE: International Reading Association.

Snow, C. E., Burns, S. M., & Griffin, P. (1998). *Preventing reading difficulties in young children*. Washington, DC: National Academics Press.

Stahl, S. A. (1992). Saying the "p" word: Nine guidelines for exemplary phonics instruction. *Reading Teacher, 45*, 618–625. Retrieved from www.jstor.org/stable/20200939

Stahl, S. A., & Murray, B. A. (1994). Defining phonological awareness and its relation to early reading. *Journal of Educational Psychology, 86*(2), 221–234. doi:10.1037/0022-0663.86.2.221

Treiman, R. (1985). Onset and rimes as units of spoken syllables: Evidence from children. *Journal of Experimental Child Psychology, 39*, 161–181. https://doi.org/10.1016/0022-0965(85)90034-7

Vloedgraven, J. M., & Verhoeven, L. (2007). Screening of phonological awareness in the early elementary grades: An IRT approach. *Annals of Dyslexia, 57*, 33–50.

Zhurova, L. S. (1963). The development of analysis of words into their sounds by preschool children. *Soviet Psychology and Psychiatry, 2*(2), 17–27. doi:10.2753/RPO1061-0405020217

Artful Teaching of Phonics

What Does Science Say About Phonics Instruction?

Artful teaching requires knowledge of how the various cognitive systems work interactively to convert written words to speech. An extraordinary body of scientific research has been accumulated over the past 50 years that has informed our understanding of the print-to-speech process. In the late 1990s, a special panel of experts was convened to evaluate reading research. This work resulted in the Report of the National Reading Panel (2000) and summarized what had been found to be important to becoming a reader. The panel used a strict set of guidelines specifying what qualified as "research" to avoid erroneous findings and arrive at defensible conclusions. Over the decades since the release of the NRP report, research has continued to not only support the findings of the panel but has provided further insight into issues of reading that were unresolved in the late 1990s. We will explore some of the critical findings from research that have important ramifications for the artful instruction of phonics instruction. Because reading is a language-based skill, we begin with a brief discussion of phonemic awareness and its role in reading. While phonemic awareness is not phonics per se, it has important implications for the success of phonics instruction.

DOI: 10.4324/9781003218609-4

Language and Reading

Most languages have an accompanying writing system that encodes spoken language into printed representations. Along with speech, the innovation of transferring speech into writing is perhaps the most profound development in human history. Think about what a writing system makes possible. It allows for the preservation of thoughts that can be recorded, stored, and shared with other people long after they originated in the mind of the writer. Some writing reflects the thoughts from people who lived thousands of years ago. However, to share in the fruits of writing requires that one be able to decipher that writing and convert it to meaning. Phonics emphasizes instruction that teaches children the connection between printed letters and their sounds that, when learned, results in pronunciation of the word (Harris & Hodges, 1995). Before we get directly into phonics, let's examine a skill or competency that precedes phonics – phonemic awareness, the ability to perceive and manipulate discreet language sounds without reference to written symbols or letters. So let's now turn our attention to the role of phonemic awareness in the print-to-speech conversion process.

 # Phonemic Awareness

An alphabetic language such as English is constructed on building blocks consisting of phonemes, morphemes, and grammar. "Reading" printed words, whether aloud or silently, begins with converting a sequence of letters (graphemes) to sounds (phonemes) that results in a word (speech). Essential to this process is the ability to 1) rapidly identify letters and their sounds and 2) distinguish between the various, connected sounds within words. If either of these skills is absent or underdeveloped, the letter-to-sound connection is broken or, at the least, suffers. Without fast and efficient letter-sound knowledge, reading will be labored, slow, and difficult for the reader because the print-to-sound conversion system is operating poorly. What has emerged from research since the 2000 NRP report is a growing consensus that phonemic awareness and letter-sound knowledge are not simply "related" to reading growth; they very likely cause reading development to occur (Clayton et al., 2020; Melby-Lervåg, Lyster, & Hulme, 2012).

An important implication then for the artful teaching of reading is that students must be explicitly taught phonemic awareness. Phonemes are the smallest unit of sound in a language and of the over 850 phonemes found in human languages, 44 of them are used in English. The English language is translucent, meaning the correspondence between letters and their sounds is often not direct. For example, consider the words *dough, cough, bough,* and *rough*. While only the initial letter is different in each word (the onset), the remainders of each word (the rime) are all pronounced quite differently. However, it is the ability to hear phonemes that enables a student to recognize the initial sound and begin the decoding process. This makes recognizing letters and their associated sounds interconnected skills and it has ramifications for teaching children the letters of the alphabet.

Alphabet Knowledge

Learning to read English begins with recognizing the 26 letters of the alphabet in both uppercase and lowercase (for example, Aa). Through practice, this recognition becomes instantaneous or "automatic," a term repeated often throughout this book. In an alphabetic system such as English, letters (called graphemes) are used to represent phonemes (Byrne, 1998). To learn to read, children must acquire the alphabetic principle, the insight or awareness that sounds are represented by letters. Alphabet knowledge acquisition means that the emerging reader can recognize the letters of the alphabet and be able to say the primary sound for each. While mastery of letters and their sounds have been shown to be critical to learning to read, it is only a first step, as many other skills must also be mastered to become a proficient reader. This does not make alphabet knowledge unimportant to reading; in fact, and as mentioned earlier, researchers are concluding that letter sound knowledge and phonemic awareness cause the development of early literacy skills (Hulme, Bower-Crane, Carroll, Duff, & Snowling, 2012). In summary, being able to both read letters and say their sounds are critical to learning to read, and skillfully teaching them together in activities that include writing results in faster learning. Teaching letter names and sounds using either a contextualized (e.g., meaning-focused activities using story or alphabet books) or decontextualized (e.g., the use of letter cards, tiles, or puzzles) approach are both effective, while the latter has been found to result in greater gains in letter sound identification and isolated letter naming (Roberts, Vadasy, & Sanders, 2020). The artful teaching of alphabet knowledge requires fundamental knowledge of the science that is reflected in pedagogy. At the same time, the judgment of the teacher is the critical, moderating factor that monitors how children respond to instruction and informs where the next step in learning must proceed.

Phonics

Here again, the NRP (2000) conducted the seminal investigation into what works for phonics. The findings of the panel were clear that *systematic* phonics instruction was superior to other approaches. Systematic instruction can be divided into three approaches. A synthetic approach teaches students to convert letters into sounds and then blend those sounds to make a word. This is often referred to as a *whole-to-part-to-whole* approach. An analytic approach teaches students to blend the onset and rime into a word using word families. The third category was not well specified by the panel but included all systematic approaches that were neither synthetic nor analytic. Of note is that the panel found that all three systematic approaches worked equally well, but this is not the end of the story.

In the past two decades, subsequent studies have found significant differences between synthetic and analytic approaches to phonics instruction. In 2004, Johnston and Watson found that a synthetic approach resulted in better phonemic awareness, spelling, and reading at the end of kindergarten. Assessing these same students seven years later, the authors found that the synthetic phonics group had better word reading and comprehension skills (Johnston, McCeown, & Watson, 2012). Two additional studies by Christensen and Bowey (2005) and de Graaf, Bosman, Hasselman, and Verhoeven (2009) also found the synthetic approach to be superior to one that is analytic. However, these results do not mean that there is no place for analytic phonics. Brady (2020) points out that the adoption of a synthetic or analytic approach is not so much an either/or decision, but more a question of when and why one should be chosen over the other.

For example, a synthetic approach is more appropriate in kindergarten for teaching alphabet knowledge and phonemic awareness where teaching needs to be very direct. On the other hand, an analytic approach may be appropriate for teaching word families in first or second grade.

A third approach to phonics instruction is to teach children to use analogies to pronounce unknown words (Goswami, 1986, 1988). For example, take a child who can pronounce the word *peak* but is unfamiliar with the word *beak*. The child can apply their understanding that the /ea/ pattern makes the long /e/ sound and apply it to the word *beak*. If *beak* is in the child's listening vocabulary, they will recognize the word upon pronunciation and confirm that they have likely said it correctly based on story context. Like in our example, analogies are very helpful at the onset and rime level. Analogies are based on the idea that children can use the similarities they see in spelling patterns to read words they do not yet know how to pronounce. In essence, children bootstrap their learning; that is, they use what they already know about words to learn more (Jorm & Share, 1983).

In the artful teaching of phonics, the teacher uses judgment based on the needs of the student to determine when to use the approach that will most benefit the student and engage them in productive instruction. The artful teacher has acquired knowledge of reading and skill with multiple instructional strategies that they can weave together as necessary to the benefit of students.

Regarding phonics instruction, research synthesized by Foorman and colleagues (2016) has congealed on several overarching concepts for teaching foundational skills across kindergarten to third grade:

1. Students need to be taught academic language, including the use of inferential and narrative language, as well as vocabulary.
2. Teach phonemic awareness and how sounds link to letters.
3. Teach students to decode words, how to analyze their parts, and to both write and recognize words.
4. Students must read connected text every day to support word identification accuracy, fluency, and comprehension.

Additionally, in some contexts, phonics instruction stops after first grade, a practice that is not supported by research. Connor and colleagues

(2007) found that regardless of a child's word reading skills, teachers who used a synthetic approach in second grade helped students become better readers. In other words, phonics instruction beyond first grade benefits all children when it is delivered systematically using a synthetic approach. Finally, approaches that incorporate writing instruction are more effective than one focused only on the teaching of phonics instruction (Ray, Dally, Colyvas, & Lane, 2021; Xue & Meisels, 2004). This is because writing builds additional and overlapping pathways in the brain, which work to strengthen phonics acquisition.

Phonics Is Developmental

Research begun in 1970 has shown that what students understand about decoding words is revealed in how they spell words (Read, 1971). This body of research is referred to as "developmental spelling," and a warning is in order at this point. Do not be misled by the use of the word *spelling*, as this has little to do with the Friday morning spelling test for which so many of us prepared by memorizing word spellings. A better descriptor and way to think about developmental spelling is as developmental *phonics* reflected by a child's spelling. Read and subsequent researchers uncovered the sequence to phonics acquisition (Gentry & Henderson, 1978; Henderson & Templeton, 1986). This scope and sequence unfolds in systematic sequences or stages that move from alphabet to pattern to meaning (Ehri, 1992; Inverzizzi & Hayes, 2004; Templeton, 1983). The first is characterized by a child's scribbling. In the second stage, letter naming (LN), the child is now learning through explicit instruction to systematically match alphabetic sounds to letters. The LN stage consists of several "features" that include short vowels, and beginning and ending consonants and their blends. It also includes what linguists call "affricates," consonants that are pronounced using a puff of air. Examples are the /j/ in *jet* and /ch/ in *choose*. Go ahead now and pronounce these two words and focus on how you make the beginning sound.

The next stage is the within-word (WW) stage. This stage is a quantum leap for the students, as where they had been focused on letter to sound connections, they must now attend to both sounds and the letter patterns within words. In this stage, long vowels reveal the world of open and closed syllables and r-controlled vowels, and other variations of consonants and vowels. The fourth stage, syllable juncture (SJ), is where the student learns how syllables are joined together by adding common inflections to single-syllable words (*make* to *making*). Students also learn how single morpheme words use vowel patterns as in *rabbit* and *motel*. Other features include prefix assimilation, where consonant doubling relies on word meaning rather than on stress or pattern.

The final stage is called derivational relationship (DR) and is where related words are derived from common root or base words. This includes silent and sounded consonants such as /g/ in *sign* and the /n/ in *column*, and words where a long vowel becomes short or changes to a schwa. An example is found in changing *define* to *definition* where the long /i/ sound in *defīne* becomes a schwa in *definətion*. Henderson and Templeton (1986) state that learning to read and spell words requires new "levels of order" (p. 314) where the student adds nuances to what they already know. This requires that students examine words to identify these orders. Early phonics instruction involves teaching students to connect letters to sounds, first at the alphabet stage, and then later by identifying sounds made by letter groups in the pattern stage. The pedagogy a teacher uses to teach phonics has its basis in how children learn and touches both science and art. This makes understanding by the teacher of how decoding knowledge unfolds in children critical so that they are more likely to learn and retain what is taught.

Research-Supported Instruction

Fundamentals of Alphabet Knowledge

Remember that artful teaching reflects the knowledge of science and instruction, and the skill at which instruction is implemented. We've discussed the important role of phonemic awareness and that it should be taught while students are learning to identify letters. Alphabet knowledge is knowing the 26 letters of the alphabet in upper- and lowercase and their associated primary sounds and lays the groundwork for letter-sound correspondence. The sequence in which letters are introduced is important, as a teacher can unintentionally create confusion for the child because of the visual and auditory similarity between letters. It cannot be assumed that curricular materials will contain a sequence that avoids these pitfalls. When choosing the order in which to teach letters, Jones and Reutzel (2012) explain that some letters have advantages that make them easier to learn than others:

1. *Own-name advantage*: Children tend to learn the letters in their name, particularly the first letter.

2. *Alphabet order advantage*: The order of letters presented in alphabet songs and books (a, b, c, d, e, f, g, and so on) means that children learn the letters at the beginning of the alphabet faster than those at the end because they had more repetition.

3. *Letter frequency advantage*: Letters that occur most often in print mean children see them more frequently which makes them easier to learn. This will be dependent on how much experience children have had with print.

4. *Letter name pronunciation advantage*: Letters that "say their own name" such as b and f are easier to learn than those that don't such as w and y.

5. *Consonant phoneme acquisition order advantage*: Consonant letters that correspond to their phonemes are learned earlier than those that don't and are easier to learn when alphabet instruction begins. For example, n, m, p, h, t, k, y, f, ng, b, d, g, w, and s are acquired early in language development while l, r, v, z, sh, ch, j, zh, and th tend to be acquired after age four (Prather, Hedrick, & Kern, 1975).

The faster children acquire alphabet knowledge, the sooner they can begin learning to blend letters into words. The "letter-a-week" method still used in some reading curricula wastes valuable learning time and should be avoided in lieu of a sequence based on what we now know about efficient learning. Although introducing new letters is contingent on the ability of students to learn them, teachers can use direct instruction with daily, distributed practice to efficiently move the process along. Also, a faster rather than slower pace to letter introduction is beneficial to all students, including those who often struggle with reading (Sunde, Furnes, & Lundetrae, 2020).

The strategy of intensive or mass practice over the course of a day is not sufficient for retention of letter sounds and names; rather, a *distributive practice* across days and weeks is a more effective practice. Cognitive science has found that distributed practice is effective for two reasons (Cepeda, Vul, Rohrer, Wixted, & Pashler, 2008). First, each time an item is successfully retrieved from memory, it becomes more resistant to being forgotten. Second, the learning context – that is, the conditions involved in the learning, such as place, environment, learner affect, and learning mode – tend to vary when practice is distributed over time. These variables can act as useful cues to later retrieval of the practiced information. Distributed learning of letters over multiple days provides the necessary reinforcement to transfer learning to long-term memory and result in the fast and accurate recall of letters and sounds. The 10/20 rule states that 10 percent to 20 percent of material that has been presented to students should be reviewed daily for long-term retention to occur (Rohrer & Pashler, 2010).

Alphabet Knowledge Instruction

When teaching letters, the fundamental learning task is to help students pair the visual letter with its name or alpha sound. A direct instruction approach to teaching alphabet knowledge is both coherent with learning science and results in the fastest acquisition by children (Roberts et al., 2020; Piasta, Purpura, & Wagner, 2010). Below is a direct instruction approach suggested by Carnine and colleagues (2006), which we have slightly modified:

1. Begin by writing the target letter on the board (let's use /m/).
2. Then say to the class, "When I touch the letter, you will say its sound. You will keep saying its sound as long as I'm touching the letter. When I take away my finger, you will stop."
3. Now model the strategy for the students: "Now listen to how I do it." Place your index finger just below the /m/ and say the letter name for two seconds by stretching the /m/ out (*mmmmmm*). Then remove your finger and stop. Repeat this several times for the students.
4. Next, do the procedure with the class by saying "Now you will pronounce /m/ with me. When I put my finger under the /m/,

pronounce its name until I take my finger away." While moving your finger to the /m/, say "What sound?" While pointing to the /m/, you and the students hold the sound "*mmmmmm*" for two seconds, then remove your finger and everyone stops saying "*mmmmmm.*"

5. Repeat the "what sound" sequence three more times so that students get four repetitions. As students practice, they become better at stopping and starting on cue.

6. Because each student must be able to correctly pronounce every letter, quickly assess each student after the lesson. This can be done with a letter card. In this case, use a lowercase /m/ on a flash card. Go to each student, hold up the card, and ask "What sound?" Be sure they respond correctly. If not, engage in several more repetitions with the student.

Phonics Instruction

A theme throughout this book is that artful instruction is authentic, aesthetic, and creative. The strategies that we present in this section, word sorts, making words, and word ladders, are "universal" strategies that can be considered artful. For example, word sorts are authentic activities engaged in by people on almost a daily basis. Sorting is used routinely to analyze and distinguish items from each other based on their characteristics (Krathwohl, 2002). All three strategies develop thinking or cognitive flexibility, an authentic characteristic of humans that is important to development (Boroditsky, Neville, Karns, Markman, & Spivey, 2010). The term "aesthetic" has broad attachments of meaning that have evolved over several centuries. One aspect of aestheticism is that it identifies the admiration of competence as a characteristic of aestheticism (Pinker, 2002). We propose that the strategies presented in this chapter help instill in the student confidence and even pleasure in the attainment of their evolving understanding and ability to unlock the code of written English. Our third term, "creative," is meant to suggest that there can be many ways to combine various instructional activities that can result in reading growth in students. These combinations can differ among teachers and ultimately reflect the individual's creativity in designing effective literacy instruction.

Word Sorts

Following letter learning, the essence of learning to decode words is connecting short sequences of those letters to sounds to read simple words (the alphabetic stage). This is followed by the recognition of letter patterns occurring within words and connecting them to sounds (pattern stage). Word sorts are a flexible, efficient, high-impact, and research-based strategy for teaching students to recognize these patterns within words (Templeton & Morris, 1999). When completing a word sort, the student is provided opportunities to recognize common spelling patterns and sounds within words, and then assign them to appropriate categories (Bear, Invernizzi, Templeton, & Johnson, 2012). Word sorts can be thought of as a universal strategy for teaching letter patterns because they are so easily adaptable. When engaged in a word sort, students use higher-order thinking skills to compare, contrast, and classify words by their letter feature patterns. Word sorts incorporate modeling, repetition, correct feedback, and reinforcement, all methods supported by a robust research base. The following steps guide the implementation of word sorts.

1. Begin by identifying the letter features targeted for learning. This can be done using a developmental spelling assessment. It is important that the chosen letter feature(s) developmentally reflect where the student is in their decoding knowledge so the sort is within the child's zone of proximal development (Vygotsky, 1978). In this example, let's assume the sort is targeting r-controlled vowels using the /ar/ letter feature. The /ar/ feature will be introduced using what the child already knows, which in this case will be the short and long /a/ as in VCe words.

2. We will make three categories of words based on their letter features: one for short /a/, a second for long /a/, and a third for /ar/, the feature to be introduced. A fourth category will be for "oddball" words that don't fit in any of the three categories.

3. Next, choose five to seven words for each of the categories. Either write or type them out on paper (card stock would add durability) and then cut them out into individual words. In our example, we'll use the words *lamp, mash, crash, band, max,* and *land* for the short /a/ feature; *grade, pace, game, save,* and *safe* for the long /a/ feature

in aCe words; and for the /ar/ feature, we'll select the words *hard*, *bark*, *car*, *lark*, *mark*, *start*, *card*, and *barn*. Finally, we'll include the word *are*, as it will not fit in any of the three categories.

4. On a piece of paper or small whiteboard, make four columns at the top, one for each letter feature as below including an "odd-ball" column for words that don't fit in the other three. Below each category header, place a box with an exemplar word inside. A sort can also be made digitally using apps such as Classkick, Seesaw, or Google Jamboard.

ă	aCe	ar	Oddball
grass	made	car	?

To implement the sort, use these steps.

1. Begin by briefly reviewing the words for meaning. Pick up a word card and ask, "What does this word mean?" If the meaning is un-known, explain the most common meaning. For example, in our selection of words, many children may not know the word *lark*, and we would tell them it is a kind of bird.

2. Next, explain the header categories to the students and how they relate to spelling and sound.

3. If students are unfamiliar with word sorts, take a word and model how to connect a word to a category. During modeling, the teacher is the only person with word cards. Take a word card, pronounce the word, and compare it to each category heading. Let's say the word on the card is *save*. Proceed by saying, "Save-grass, save-made, save-car. I think it's a long /a/ sound and goes in the aCe column under *made*."

4. Proceed by giving students one word at a time and have them place it in the correct category.

5. Once the sort is complete, an important part is to engage the students in an analysis of the sort. Questions like "What do you notice about all the words under grass?" or "Why didn't the word

card go in the short a category?" can be asked. The point is to engage students in thinking about the relationships among the various features.

Word sorts work well for all students, including English language learners, because it allows students to use phonics in the context of words, leverages inquiry learning, and is hands-on instruction.

Making Words

Do you recall as a student yourself that a common activity used by teachers in many elementary classrooms was to put a word on display on the board – say *baseball*. Then, for ten minutes or so, students were given the task of making as many words as they could out of the letters in *baseball*. At the end of the time period, students called out the words they made and the student with the most words or the longest word was declared the winner. We have met many adults who recall doing this activity and actually enjoying it. It was fun to try to make words.

However, such an approach did not involve any actual instruction on the part of the teacher. Students worked independently, and those students who struggled in reading probably found it frustrating and did not benefit from it at all.

Patricia Cunningham took that age-old and enjoyable activity for some students and flipped it so that a teacher could guide students in making words. Instead of starting with a word, such as *baseball*, Cunningham's approach, termed Making Words, started with the students having the individual letters in *baseball* (a, a, e and b, b, l, l, s) and guiding students to make a series of words predetermined by the teacher. The final word in the lesson was a word that used every letter and made the activity gamelike.

This activity aims to help students connect the relationships between letters and sounds that has significant evidence supporting its use is Making Words (Cunningham, 2000, 2006, 2007; Cunningham & Cunningham, 1992) and Making and Writing Words (Rasinski & Oswald, 2005). In this 15-minute, hands-on activity, children are given a set of curated letters that they can use to spell about 12 to 15 words. For early readers, these may be two-letter words that grow to four- and five-letter words and longer as they progress. For very early readers still working on alphabet knowledge, letters include those they have been taught and are currently learning. Like word sorts, Making Words helps students become aware of the sounds and patterns within words by unlocking the many ways that English spelling works, where changing even a single letter can completely change the pronunciation of a word.

To implement a Making Words lesson, begin with the end in mind – the words you want children to spell. Of course, not just any words will do. This is where the artful teacher bridges the distance between science and teaching. Reading research, particularly developmental spelling, has identified the general sequence that children progress through when learning to read words. Using this critical knowledge, the teacher can target the specific letter features that children have learned for which reinforcement would be beneficial. Also, features within the child's developmental reach may also be appropriate. What should be avoided are words with features that are beyond the developmental reach of the child. Let's look at an example.

Ms. Connolly has a group of second grade students whose letter feature knowledge is nearing the end of the within-word stage. In this stage, readers become attuned to the spelling patterns inside words, including VCe patterns; r-controlled vowels; long vowel patterns such as aCe, ai, ea, and ee; complex consonant patterns such as final /k/, /ch/, silent consonants, and soft /c/ and /g/; and abstract vowels such as /ou/ and /ow/. Combining her knowledge of spelling development with what her assessment has shown her students need to learn, she has decided to design a Making Words lesson to focus on words containing the letter features /aw/ and /ow/. There are three major steps to a Making Words lesson:

1. Students manipulate letters to spell words.
2. Students sort words according to their rhyming pattern.
3. Students use the words they know to read two new words.

Ms. Connolly works through the following steps to implement her Making Words lesson:

Preparation for Making Words

1. Since Ms. Connolly knows she wants students to practice with the letter features /aw/ and /ow/, she chooses words containing

those letter features. Ms. Connolly chooses the words *was, saw, law, low, now, snow, slow, ball, allow,* and *snowball.* She selects *snowball* because it contains the necessary letters to spell each of the other words and it becomes the secret word students will spell. Ms. Connolly now knows she needs each of the letters in *snowball* for the activity.

2. To implement the activity, each student needs a baggie containing letter cards for each of the letters in *snowball*. Ms. Connolly can either purchase ready-made letter cards or use cardstock to make letter cards by printing the lowercase letter on one side and the uppercase letter on the other side. Since she is planning this as a small-group activity, Ms. Connolly make five sets of letter cards.

Step One: Making Words

3. To begin the activity, Ms. Connolly gathers four students at a table and gives each student a baggie and then asks them to remove the *o* and *w*. She explains that these two letters work together to make the sound heard in the words *now* and *slow*. Students pronounce both words with Ms. Connolly.

4. Students then take the letters *w, a,* and *s*. Ms. Connolly uses the word *was* in a sentence by saying "I *was* going to the store." Students are then directed to spell the word *saw*.

5. By changing one letter, students now spell *law*. "The *law* says we must stop our car at red lights."

6. By changing one letter in *law*, students spell *low*. "The water in the river is *low*."

7. Students change the initial consonant in *low* to spell *now*. "I want to go *now*."

8. Adding *s* to *now* spells *snow*. "It will probably *snow* tonight."

9. Change one letter in *snow* to spell *slow*. "That car is going *slow*."

10. Three new letters are used to spell *ball*. "She threw the *ball*."

11. Now students spell the five-letter word *allow*. "The principal said I cannot *allow* that."

12. Ms. Connolly now arrives at the secret word that uses all the letters. She gives the students a clue by saying, "It's a compound word and we've already made two of the words." With no correct answers, she says, "It begins with *sn*." One student says, "It's *snowball*. She threw a *snowball*." Each student now spells *snowball*.

Step Two: Sort the Words

The next step is to sort the ten words by their rhyming patterns (/as/, /ow/, /aw/). Ms. Connolly asks, "What are the two rhyming patterns in the words you spelled?" A student responds that they are /aw/ and /ow/. Ms. Connolly leads the students in pronouncing each of the words and then asks them to sort the words into groups that rhyme. This results in the following groups:

/aw/		/ow/
saw	Slow	allow
law	Low	now
	Snow	

Ms. Connolly points out that /ow/ makes two different sounds.

Step Three: Transfer

Ms. Connolly shows the students two new words: – *show* and *plow* – and explains that it's hard to tell which sound the /ow/ makes. When they come to these words in a sentence, they can try the word both ways and then decide which one makes sense. She tries each word in a sentence with the students:

Ms. Connolly reads the sentence, "I want to *show* you my new puppy" by applying the /ow/ sound in *allow* to the word *show*. She reads it again and this time applies the /ow/ sound in *slow* to *show* and now students recognize the word. Ms. Connolly uses the same method to explain how to pronounce the word *plow* in the sentence "He will *plow* the field before winter."

Adaptation

Rasinski and Oswald (2005) adapted Making Words into an alternative version called Making and Writing Words. Instead of students manipulating individual letter tiles, they are guided in actually writing the words they make on a form. The use of this approach increases the ease of employment of the activity as the teacher only needs to copy one form to be used for every student. Moreover, the students are involved in actually writing the words as they are made, thus adding a kinesthetic dimension to the activity and allowing for the improvement of student handwriting.

Word Ladders – Another Word-Building Game

As adults, most of us enjoy playing board games and the like with family and friends. It's a very authentic activity in our lives. Have you ever noticed how many of these games are word games? In our own circle of family and friends, we have enjoyed playing Scrabble, Boggle, Balderdash, Wheel of Fortune, Code Word, and many others. If we enjoy playing games as adults, why wouldn't children in school? And, in fact, many creative teachers find ways to bring gamelike activities into their classrooms. But oftentimes, those games are reserved for only when the "real work" of school is completed. And students who struggle in reading are often the ones who don't get the work done. They are often the ones who miss out on the fun. How sad.

McCandliss, Beck, Sandak, and Perfetti (2003) describe a different word-building activity in which students are guided in making a series of words, using letter tiles, by changing, adding, subtracting, or rearranging one or more letters in going from one word to another. For example, students would start with the word *stop*, take away one letter to make *top*, rearrange the letters to make *pot*, change the vowel to make *pet*, and finish by changing one letter to make *pen*. Throughout the activity, the teacher points out individual letters, sounds, letter-sound positions, and word meanings as students build their words. In their scientific study of this activity, McCandliss and colleagues found that struggling first grade students in this intervention exhibited greater growth in standardized measures of phonemic awareness, word decoding, and comprehension over a comparison group of students.

Rasinski (2005, 2008) adapted this word-building approach into a gamelike activity by having the first and last words in the "word ladder" be related in some way. For example, start with the word *kin* and work down:

kin Meaning family. Students would then be directed to make the following words:

king (add one letter to *kin*)

sing (change one letter in *king*)

sting (add one letter to *sing*)

tin (take away two letters from *sting*)

ton (change one letter in *tin*)

top (change one letter in *ton*)

pop (change one letter in *top*)

pup (change the vowel in *pop*)

pump (add one letter to *pup*)

Combine the first and last words to make *pumpkin*!

By creatively adding a gamelike dimension to the scientifically validated McCandliss et al. (2003) activity, Rasinski made the instruction artful as well as scientific.

In this chapter, we have briefly reviewed some of the science regarding the teaching of phonics. We then discussed one strategy for teaching alphabet knowledge and several activities for teaching letter feature knowledge. All the strategies are based on reading science and what we know about how children learn. The artful teacher can apply these various strategies to foster what students need to learn about reading in an aesthetic way that keeps them both engaged in instruction and positively motivated about reading. Of course, there are other strategies beyond those we have highlighted that engage the creative, authentic, and aesthetic aspects of great teaching that we hope you will explore.

References

Bear, D. R., Invernizzi, M. A., Templeton, S., & Johnston, F. (2012). *Words their way: Word study for phonics, vocabulary and spelling instruction* (5th ed.). Boston: Pearson.

Boroditsky, L., Neville, H., Karns, C., Markman, A. B., & Spivey, M. J. (2010). Flux: Fundamental or frivolous? In S. Ohlsson & R. Catrambone (Eds.), *Proceedings of the 32nd annual meeting of the cognitive science society* (pp. 2918–2919). Austin, TX: Cognitive Science Society.

Brady, S. (2020). A 2020 perspective on research findings on alphabetics (phoneme awareness and phonics): Implications for instruction. *The Reading League Journal, 1*(3), 20–28.

Byrne, B. (1998). *The foundation of literacy: The child's acquisitions of the alphabetic principle*. Hove, England: Psychology Press.

Carnine, D. W., Silbert, J., Kame'enui, E. J., Tarver, S. G., & Jungjohann, K. (2006). *Teaching struggling and at-risk readers: A direct instruction approach*. Upper Saddle River, NJ: Pearson.

Cepeda, N. J., Vul, E., Rohrer, D., Wixted, J. T., & Pashler, H. (2008). Spacing effects in learning: A temporal ridgeline of optimal retention. *Psychological Science, 19*(11), 1095–1102. https://doi.org/10.1111%2Fj.1467-9280.2008.02209.x

Christensen, C., & Bowey, J. (2005). The efficacy of orthographic rime, grapheme-phoneme correspondence and explicit approaches to teaching decoding skills. *Scientific Studies of Reading, 9*(4), 91–107. https://doi.org/10.1207/s1532799xssr0904_1

Clayton, F. J., West, G., Sear, C., Hulme, C., & Lervåg, A. (2020). A longitudinal study of early reading development: Letter-sound knowledge, phoneme awareness and RAN, but not letter-sound integration, predict variations in reading development. *Scientific Studies of Reading, 24*(2), 91–107. https://doi.org/10.1080/10888438.2019.1622546

Connor, C., Morrison, F., & Underwood, P. S. (2007). A second chance in second grade: The independent and cumulative impact of first and second grade reading instruction and students' letter-word reading skill growth. *Scientific Studies of Reading, 11*(3), 199–233. https://doi.org/10.1080/10888430701344314

Cunningham, P. M. (2000). *Systematic sequential phonics they use*. Greensboro, NC: Carson-Dellosa Publishing.

Cunningham, P. M. (2006). High-poverty schools that beat the odds. *The Reading Teacher, 60*, 382–385. https://doi.org/10.1598/RT.60.4.9

Cunningham, P. M. (2007). Six successful high poverty schools: How they beat the odds. In D. W. Rowe, R. T. Jimenez, D. L. Compton, D. K.

Dickinson, Y. Kim, K. M. Leander, & V. J. Risko (Eds.), *56th yearbook of the national reading conference* (pp. 191–203). Milwaukee, WI: National Reading Conference.

Cunningham, P. M., & Cunningham, J. W. (1992). Making words: Enhancing the invented spelling-decoding connection. *The Reading Teacher, 46*(2), 106–115.

deGraaff, S., Bosman, A. M. T., Hasselman, F., & Verhoeven, L. (2009). Benefits of systematic phonics instruction. *Scientific Studies of Reading, 13*(4), 318–333.

Ehri, L. C. (1992). Review and commentary: Stages of development spelling. In S. Templeton & D. R. Bear (Eds.), *Development of orthographic knowledge and the foundation of literacy: A memorial festschrift for Edmund H. Henderson* (pp. 307–332). Hillsdale, NJ: Erlbaum.

Foorman, B., Beyler, N., Borradaile, K., Coyne, M., Denton, C. A., et al. (2016). *Foundational skills to support reading for understanding in kindergarten through 3rd grade (NCEE 2016–4008)*. Washington, DC: National Center for Education Evaluation and Regional Assistance (NCEE), Institute of Education Sciences, U.S. Department of Education. http://whatworks.ed.govhttps://doi.org/10.1080/10888430903001308

Gentry, J. R., & Henderson, E. H. (1978). Three steps to teaching beginning readers to spell. *The Reading Teacher, 31*(6), 632–637.

Goswami, U. (1986). Children's use of analogy in learning to read: A developmental study. *Journal of Experimental Child Psychology, 42,* 73–83. https://doi.org/10.1016/0022-0965(86)90016-0

Goswami, U. (1988). Orthographic analogies and reading development. *Quarterly Journal of Experimental Psychology: Human Experimental Psychology, 40*(A), 239–268. https://doi.org/10.1080/02724988430 00113

Harris, T. L., & Hodges, R. E. (1995). *The literacy dictionary*. Newark, DE: International Reading Association.

Henderson, E. H., & Templeton, S. (1986). A developmental perspective of formal spelling instruction through alphabet, pattern, and meaning. *The Elementary School Journal, 86*(3), 304–316. https://doi.org/10.1086/461451

Hulme, C., Bower-Crane, C., Carroll, J. M., Duff, F. J., & Snowling, M. J. (2012). The causal role of phonemic awareness and letter-sound knowledge in learning to read: Combining intervention studies with mediation analysis. *Psychological Science, 26*(6), 572–577. https://doi.org/10.1177%2F0956797611435921

Inverzizzi, M., & Hayes, L. (2004). Developmental spelling research: A systematic imperative. *Reading Research Quarterly, 39*(2), 216–228. https://doi.org/10.1598/RRQ.39.2.4

Johnston, R. S., McCeown, S., & Watson, J. E. (2012). Long-term effects of synthetic versus analytic phonics teaching on the reading and spelling ability of 10 year old boys and girls. *Reading and Writing: An Interdisciplinary Journal, 25*, 1365–1384.

Johnston, R. S., & Watson, J. E. (2004). Accelerating the development of reading, spelling, and phonemic awareness skills in initial readers. *Reading and Writing: An Interdisciplinary Journal, 17*(4), 327–357.

Jones, C. D., & Reutzel, D. R. (2012). Enhanced alphabet knowledge: Exploring a change of frequency, focus, and distributed cycles or review. *Reading Psychology, 33*(5), 448–464. https://doi.org/10.1080/02702711.2010.545260

Jorm, A. F., & Share, D. L. (1983). Phonological recoding and reading acquisition. *Applied Psycholinguistics, 4*, 103–147.

Krathwohl, D. (2002). A revision of Bloom's taxonomy: An overview. *Theory into Practice, 41*(4), 212–218. https://doi.org/10.1207/s15430421tip4104_2

McCandliss, B., Beck, I., Sandak, R., & Perfetti, C. (2003). Focusing attention on decoding for children with poor reading skills: Design and preliminary tests of the word building intervention. *Scientific Studies in Reading, 7*, 75–104.

Melby-Lervåg, M., Lyster, S. H., & Hulme, C. (2012). Phonological skills and their role in learning to read: A meta-analytic review. *Psychological Review, 138*(2), 322–352. https://psycnet.apa.org/doi/10.1037/a0026744

National Reading Panel. (2000). *Teaching children to read: An evidence-based assessment of the scientific research literature on reading and its implications for reading instruction. National institute of health pub. No. 00–4769*. Washington, DC: National Institute of Child Health and Human Development.

Piasta, S. B., Purpura, D. J., & Wagner, R. K. (2010). Fostering alphabet knowledge development: A comparison of two instructional approaches. *Reading and Writing, 23*(6), 607–626.

Pinker, D. (2002). *The blank slate: The modern denial of human nature.* New York: Penguin Books.

Prather, E. M., Hedrick, D. L., & Kern, C. A. (1975). Articulation development in children aged two to four years. *Journal of Speech and Hearing Disorders, 40,* 179–191. https://doi.org/10.1044/jshd.4002.179

Rasinski, T. (2005). *Daily word ladders, grades 2–3.* New York: Scholastic.

Rasinski, T. (2008). *Daily word ladders, grades 1–2.* New York: Scholastic.

Rasinski, T., & Oswald, R. (2005). Making and writing words: Constructivist word learning in a second-grade classroom. *Reading and Writing Quarterly, 21*(2), 151–163. doi:10.1080/10573560590915950

Ray, K., Dally, K., Colyvas, K., & Lane, A. E. (2021). The effects of a whole-class kindergarten handwriting intervention on early reading skills. *Reading Research, Quarterly,* 1–15. https://doi.org/10.1002/rrq.395

Read, C. (1971). Pre-school children's knowledge of English phonology. *Harvard Educational Review, 41*(1), 1–54.

Roberts, T. A., Vadasy, P. F., & Sanders, E. A. (2020). Preschool instruction in letter names and sounds: Does contextualized or decontextualized instruction matter? *Reading Research Quarterly, 55*(4), 573–600. https://doi.org/10.1002/rrq.284

Rohrer, D., & Pashler, H. (2010). Recent research on human learning challenges conventional instructional strategies. *Educational Researcher, 39*(5), 406–412. https://doi.org/10.3102%2F0013189X10374770

Sunde, K., Furnes, B., & Lundetrae, K. (2020). Does introducing the letters faster boost the development children's letter knowledge, word reading, and spelling in the first year of school? *Scientific Studies of Reading, 24*(2), 141–158. https://doi.org/10.1080/10888438.2019.16 15491

Templeton, S. (1983). Using the spelling/meaning connection to develop word knowledge in older students. *Journal of Reading, 27*(1), 8–14. Retrieved from www.jstor.org/stable/40029290

Templeton, S., & Morris, D. (1999). Theory and research into practice: Questions teachers ask about spelling. *Reading Research Quarterly, 34*(1), 102–112, 151–218.

Vygotsky, L. S. (1978). *Mind in society: The development of higher psychological processes* (M. Cole, V. John-Steiner, S. Scribner, & E. Souberman, Eds.). Cambridge, MA: Harvard University Press.

Xue, Y., & Meisels, S. J. (2004). Early literacy instruction and learning in kindergarten: Evidence from the early childhood longitudinal study – kindergarten class of 1998–1999. *American Educational Research Journal, 41*(1), 191–229. https://doi.org/10.3102%2F00028312041001191

5 | Artful Teaching of Reading Fluency

It's Friday afternoon and Mr. Takata's third grade class is full of anticipation getting ready for the weekly poetry slam. Tables and desks are rearranged to create a performance area in the front of the room. Other chairs are brought in to accommodate guests. Shades on the windows are drawn, overhead lights are dimmed, and a lamp on Mr. T's desk is lit to create just the right mood for students to perform the poetry they have been rehearsing all week long.

The last 30 minutes of almost every Friday in this class is reserved for Takata's Poetry Slam. Although a poetry slam is typically a competition, in Mr. T's class, the title of "poetry slam" is simply used to note the specialness of the activity in which students read and perform poetry with expression and enthusiasm. Parents are invited for this weekly event, and it is not unusual for the school principal and other members of the school community to attend the slam.

Mr. T begins every slam by giving a brief background and overview to the day's performances – for this day, students have been studying, rehearsing, and will be performing the poetry of a renowned children's poet, David Harrison. After Mr. T's introduction, students come up, individually, in pairs, in trios, and in even larger groups to perform the poem they have selected from Harrison's books of poetry that are on display in the classroom. Each reading performance is followed by gentle applause and finger snapping, as well as positive comments by audience members about the readings. Each Friday, students leave the school with a feeling of accomplishment and a job well done.

This poetry slam is really the "icing on the cake" that follows some intensive, authentic, and artful fluency work that was done earlier in the

DOI: 10.4324/9781003218609-5

week. In Mr. Takata's class, every Monday, students are given the opportunity to select poems (or other performance texts such as songs, speeches, or segments of speeches or scripts) that they would like to learn to read fluently and perform on Fridays. Students also determine if they want to work solo on their texts or work with any classmates. Then, throughout the week in the classroom and at home, students rehearse their assigned texts. Students have a natural purpose for learning to read their text fluently, as they will be performing it on Friday to an audience of peers, family members, and others.

As a person who has performed his own poetry at coffee houses and other venues, Mr. Takata is familiar with the notion of poetry performances. He found such value and enjoyment in these experiences that he decided to bring it into his own classroom. And the work has paid off – students' fluency, as measured by reading rate and oral reading expression, has improved significantly over the course of the year.

> Parents are constantly remarking to me how much their students' oral reading fluency has improved. Comprehension, too, seems to have improved as students engage in discussion on how poems and texts should be performed in order to make meaningful and satisfying performances for their audience.

Equally important for Mr. Takata is the increase in confidence students have in themselves as readers and also their appreciation of the poetry and other texts they read.

> It's amazing to see how my students have changed over the year. Early in the year, they would be hunched over or would lean on the wall when performing and in some cases read in such a low voice it was difficult to audience members to actually hear what was being read. Now in April, they know that in order to give a good performance they need to stand straight and tall and read with a voice that can be heard throughout the classroom. As I often tell my students, "When in doubt, shout!" And they do.

What Is Fluency and Why Is It Important?

For years, reading fluency was a relatively unknown or, at best, ignored competency in reading. It was most commonly associated with oral reading, and since most reading we do as adults is not oral but silent, fluency was not viewed as all that important. However, in the 1980s, scientific research and scholarly writing began to focus on the concept of reading fluency. The first task was to actually define what is meant by "reading fluency."

Fluency – Automaticity in Word Recognition

On the surface, the notion of fluency implies doing something with ease or as in a flow. Researchers such as David LaBerge and Jay Samuels (1974) described this notion of ease or flow in word recognition as automaticity – the ability to read the words in a text not just accurately, as is often the goal in phonics instruction, but also automatically or effortlessly. As you read this chapter, you are probably doing so automatically. How often do you have to stop to analyze or sound out any of the words in this paragraph? Very few, we suppose. Perhaps the word *automaticity* may have caused you to stop for a second, as it is a word you may not be familiar with.

The significance of automaticity in reading lies in the fact that the act of reading itself requires multitasking. At the very least, readers must decode (and understand) the words they encounter in any text read, and they must also work to construct meaning of the text. Pair this with the notion that all readers have a limited amount of attention or cognitive energy that they can devote to the act of reading. If readers have to devote too much of their attention to the word-decoding aspect of reading, they will not have a sufficient amount remaining for the more important task of constructing meaning or comprehension. Think of those students who read in an overly labored word-by-word manner, often having to stop to analyze and sound out individual words. These students' comprehension will likely be compromised, as most of their effort is devoted to word decoding, not making meaning.

Word recognition automaticity solves the multitasking problem inherent in reading. When a reader is able to automatically recognize the words in a text, they are able to minimize the effort given to word decoding and maximize their cognitive energy to be devoted to comprehension. So even though word recognition automaticity is an action devoted to recognizing the words in a passage, the end result of automaticity is improved reading comprehension.

Scientific studies have regularly demonstrated a significant and substantial relationship between word recognition automaticity and comprehension and overall reading proficiency. In a study of nearly 2,000 fourth grade students conducted by the National Assessment of Educational Progress (McKenzie, McGhee, & Reid, 2019), students who were determined to be at the lowest levels of reading achievement were found to also have the lowest levels of word recognition automaticity as measured by reading rate. With every higher level of reading achievement came a corresponding improvement in word recognition automaticity. Thus, the implication of this and many other studies is that improving word recognition automaticity will improve comprehension and overall reading achievement.

So how does one develop automaticity in anything? The answer is practice. If you practice an action or activity enough times, you develop automatic control over that action or activity. Think of how effortful it was when you first learned to drive a car. All your attention had to be given to controlling and operating your car. However, with practice, your ability to drive became more automatic. In fact, if you are a fairly experienced driver, you can usually multitask while driving. You can listen to the radio or converse with a passenger or think about your plans for the day while still safely driving the car.

Fluency – Prosody

One of the things that makes the concept of reading fluency a bit muddled is that there is another part to reading fluency that also began to get the attention of reading scholars and researchers (for example, Schreiber, 1980) in the 1970s and '80s. It is the concept of "prosody." Prosody is a linguistic term and refers to the melodic or expressive part of speech or oral reading. When we speak with an acquaintance, we communicate meaning not just with the words that come out of our mouths, but in the way we say those words – we raise and lower the pitch of our voices, we emphasize certain words, we speed up in some places but slow down in others, we insert dramatic pauses in our speech, and we phrase our speech into chunks of words that are separated by pauses. All these prosodic actions help to communicate meaning to a listener. Indeed, when we think about people who are fluent speakers, we often think of them as folks who use their voices to communicate meaning.

The same is true in reading, except the listener in the reading act is the same person who is doing the reading. In essence, the reader is helping to communicate meaning to herself or himself when reading orally or even when reading silently. Most people admit that when they read silently, they still hear that internal voice.

Research has shown that readers who read orally with good expression tend to be good comprehenders when reading silently. Indeed, the same NAEP study of fourth graders mentioned earlier found that students at the lowest levels of reading proficiency also were rated lowest in terms of their oral reading expressiveness. With every increase in reading proficiency came a corresponding increase in oral reading expressiveness. Again, the implication from this is that one way to improve students' reading proficiency is to improve their oral reading prosody or expressiveness.

How does one improve expressiveness in reading? Again, the answer is practice. Through the act of reading itself, readers become better able to make voices, oral and silent, sound like authentic language. Certain kinds of practice, however, seem to be particularly well suited for improving both automaticity and prosody. We will discuss these later in this chapter.

Fluency – The Bridge from Word Recognition to Comprehension

Some readding scholars have called fluency a link from word recognition to comprehension. Automaticity is half of the bridge that links to word recognition itself. We want students to be not just accurate in their decoding of words but also automatic. The second half of the bridge is prosody. It is not enough for readers to decode the words in text accurately and automatically; they also need to read them with good expression and phrasing that reflects the meaning of the text. Think about it – in order to read a text with appropriate expression, you need to be making and monitoring the meaning of the text itself.

Students who struggle in reading seem to have considerable difficulty in crossing this fluency bridge to comprehension. A study of third and fourth grade students who performed poorly on state mandated tests of silent reading proficiency found that a substantial number of these students exhibit difficulties in one or both areas of fluency – automaticity and prosody (Valencia & Buly, 2004). However, although we may think of the development of reading fluency as something that occurs in the elementary grades, research has shown that students in the middle and secondary grades who struggle in reading manifest difficulties with fluency (Paige, Magpuri-Lavell, Rasinski, & Smith, 2013; Paige, Rasinski, & Magpuri-Lavell, 2012; Rasinski et al., 2005). The upshot of this research is that reading fluency is important at all grade levels and especially for students who are not proficient readers.

The Science of Teaching Reading Fluency

So, what are the tools that teachers have at their disposal for developing fluency in students? Science and scholarly thought (Rasinski, 2010) have identified a set of instructional tools that can be used to create instruction that is effective in developing fluency.

Model Fluent Reading

In order for students to know what fluent reading is, they need to hear it. They need to hear their teachers and others read to them regularly in voices that are expressive and meaningful. The importance of reading aloud to students has been a mainstay of reading curricula for many generations. Here's what we know about reading to students.

Reading aloud to students builds knowledge in students of the content that is being read. The importance of background knowledge (or "schema," as it is called in more intellectual circles) for reading is huge. Readers are more likely to understand a text if they have some knowledge of the topic at hand. Reading to students is an excellent way to provide that knowledge. Additionally, because we can read to students material that is above their own reading level, reading to students provides opportunities to improve students' overall comprehension development and increase their vocabularies (higher level texts have more challenging words in context that will increase students' vocabularies).

Students who are read to generally have a better attitude toward reading than students who are not read to. To this day, all of us (your authors) love to be read to or to listen to a book or other text that is recorded so that we can listen to it on our phones or in our cars. Being read to, especially when the person is reading in a fluent manner, is an enjoyable experience. Many students who struggle in reading do not like reading. Reading to students is one way to overcome this hurdle.

Finally, reading to students helps students develop a metacognitive sense of what constitutes fluent reading. It gives students a fluency goal to aim for in their own reading. This is especially true if the teacher or person reading to students will occasionally talk about how their reading is fluent and what they had to do (rehearse) in order to get their reading to the point where the reading was fluent.

Reading with Students – Assisted Reading

When students listen to someone read to them, they are listening, not reading. Although read aloud helps students develop a sense for the nature of fluent reading, they need to actually do the reading in order to move toward fluency. Yet students who are just moving into fluency reading may not be able to read a text fluently on their own.

The answer to this dilemma is to have students read with the assistance of one or more voices who also read the text. We call this "assisted reading," as the other more fluent voices are providing a scaffold or support that allows the student to be successful and move toward fluency. Regardless of type of assisted reading used in the classroom, home, or other setting, the research is clear – students who regularly engage in assisted reading improve their oral fluency and are more likely to improve their overall reading proficiency (Rasinski, Reutzel, Chard, & Linan-Thompson, 2011).

Assisted reading can take a variety of forms. Perhaps the most common form of assisted reading is choral reading where students read as part of a group – classmates, teacher, others. The multitude of voices allows for each reader to support the group. And if a text is read chorally multiple times, students will eventually reach a point where they can read the text independently and fluently. Choral reading can take a variety of forms: whole-group choral reading, echo choral reading, and antiphonal choral reading, in which parts are broken up for subgroups of readers.

Paired or duolog reading is choral reading with two readers: the developing reader and a more fluent proficient reader. In paired reading, the two readers sit side by side and read the same text aloud together. The more proficient reader adjusts their reading rate to accommodate the student. The student actually controls the reading, as they can determine when or if they want to try solo reading for a while with simply a tap on the wrist of the more proficient partner. When this happens, the partner reads along silently until cued again by the student to join in or when the student begins to experience difficulty in their solo oral reading.

Recorded Reading

Reading while listening to a prerecorded and fluent reading of a text is another form of assisted reading. The student is hearing a fluent rendering of a text while simultaneously reading on their own. This form of assisted reading is particularly helpful for students who may wish to have a degree of privacy in their oral reading. Recorded reading can be done in private. The key to recorded reading, however, is to ensure that the student is actually reading and not simply listening to the text being read and performed. If the student is only listening, they may enjoy a good story or learn some knowledge but will likely not improve their own reading fluency.

Practice – Wide Reading

How does one become fluent at anything? Of course, the obvious answer, yet again, is practice. "Practice makes perfect" is more than just a cliché; there is much truth in those three words. In reading, when we think of practice, we often think of wide reading. Wide reading is the kind of reading most of us do as adults – it simply means reading one text after another. Once you finish one book read for pleasure or an article in a magazine, you move on to the next book or passage.

Clearly, wide reading is important for the development of many aspects of reading besides fluency. Research has clearly demonstrated a strong correlation between the amount of reading and reading achievement. The implication is clear – the more students read the more likely they are to be proficient readers (Allington & McGill-Franzen, 2021). The challenge for teachers is how to get students to increase their reading volume. Certainly, incentives (rewards) can motivate students to read in the short run. But for long-term change, we need to find ways to help students see the intrinsic value and satisfaction that reading can provide. That is the art of teaching reading. And certainly, reading to students material that they would find interesting and providing students with time in the school day (and at home) for independent reading are great ways to move students toward a reading life.

Practice – Repeated Reading

Wide reading generally suggests one reading of a text and then moving on to another text. However, for younger and struggling readers, or when reading a text that is challenging, one reading may not be enough. In cases such as these, two or even more readings may be necessary to achieve fluency and comprehension of a text. We have come to call this form of reading practice "repeated readings."

One of the first mentions of the concept of repeated readings in the scientific and professional literacy journals came in an article in the journal *The Reading Teacher* that was aptly named "The Method of Repeated Readings" by S. Jay Samuels (1979). In this paper, Samuels describe a method of reading instruction where students were asked to read a text multiple times until they achieved a relatively high level of fluency. Of course, with every successive reading, students improved in their reading performance. However, the exciting finding was that when students move on to new texts they had never read before, there were vestiges of improved fluency on this new reading. In other words, repeated practice of one text resulted in generalized improvements in fluency beyond the original text – real learning occurred through repeated reading. This finding has been corroborated in many subsequent studies with students of various ages and levels of reading fluency. Thus, we can say without hesitation that repeated readings of texts has been validated by science.

Of course, the next question, as with wide reading, is how can teachers engage students in reading text multiple times? Now, in many classrooms around the country, well-meaning teachers have students read a text multiple times for the purpose of reading it more quickly than the time before (that is, to improve a measure of word recognition automaticity). We feel that this is an inauthentic way to engage in repeated reading. Where in real life do people engage in reading a text more than one time for the purpose of reading it fast? We can't think of any. Finding authentic ways to engage in repeated reading is the challenge posed by the art of teaching reading and will be addressed later in this chapter.

Phrase-Cue Text

A hallmark of disfluent reading is reading in a word-by-word manner in a monotone or near monotone voice. It doesn't take long to determine if such a reader is struggling with fluency. Proficient and fluent readers read in chunks or phrases, while less fluent readers do not. Meaning tends to lie in phrases rather than individual words. For example, words such as *if, of, the, am,* and *with* have little meaning by themselves. They need to read as part of a phrase or sentence – "if you do this," "a friend of mine," "the big dog," and "I am with him." Helping students move from less fluent to more fluent reading can be done by providing explicit cueing of phrases for students who may have not yet achieved this ability on their own. In essence, the notion of phrase-cued texts allows students to phrase a text into meaningful chunks before they have the ability to do it on their own. In a review of research on phrase-cued texts, Rasinski (1990) found that three-quarters of the studies reported positive effects for cueing or marking phrase boundaries for students at a variety of grade levels. The improvement, by the way, went beyond fluency and included improvements in reading comprehension.

There is no one way to phrase-cue a text. Again, this is where the art of teaching comes in – the teacher determines the way that is optimal for their students. The cueing could be in the form of marking the text with a line (scoops) under the phrase (and having students do the same with new texts), slash marks inserted into a text, or even color-coding phrases. No matter how the phrase-cueing is done, the key is to make explicit for students that which they have not yet mastered.

Synergistic Fluency Instruction

The elements of fluency instruction described above individually work to promote fluency development in students. However, when we combine these individual instructional elements into an instructional package or routine, we get what can be termed "synergy." Essentially, synergy means that the effects of combining the individual elements leads to positive effects for students that are greater than the sum of the individual parts. In other words, the various individual elements reinforce and amplify one another so that a larger instructional effect is manifested in students. In the sections below, we describe two forms of synergistic fluency instruction that we have developed and researched.

The Fluency Development Lesson

The Fluency Development Lesson (FDL) (Rasinski, Padak, Linek, & Sturtevant, 1994) was developed as a regularly implemented fluency lesson provided to large groups of normally developing students or as a more intensive intervention to smaller groups of students who struggle in fluency and overall reading achievement. The FDL is a daily lesson in which students are tasked with mastering to the point of fluent reading a new relatively short (100 to 200 words) text each day. In other words, the goal for the lesson is for students to achieve success in fluent reading with every lesson. The lesson takes approximately 20 to 25 minutes and can be implemented with classroom groups, small groups, or even individual students. Throughout any part of the FDL, the focus is on developing automatic and expressive oral reading, not fast reading. The general daily protocol for the FDL involves the following steps:

1. In preparation for the lesson, the teacher selects a text for the day. The text can be a passage from a story, an informational piece, a poem, or a song – the key is to keep the text relatively short, as students will be reading it several times. The texts should be at or slightly above the students' instructional reading level and should be a reading with good phrasing and expression. Two copies of the

text are made for every student. Additionally, a larger display copy of the text is made for group reading.

2. Modeling Fluent Reading. The teacher introduces the display copy of the text to students and reads it to them multiple times while the students follow along silently on the display copy of the text or on their own individual copies. The teacher can vary the way they read the text in order for students to note variation in expression or lack of expression.

3. Following the teacher's multiple readings, the students and teacher engage in a brief discussion of the content of the text as well as the nature of the teacher's oral reading. Which part of teacher's reading was the best and why?

4. Assisted Reading. Next, the teacher and students read the display copy of the text two to three times using various forms of choral reading. The choral readings can change from the whole-group reading to echo reading to having different subgroups read the passage.

5. Assisted Repeated Reading. Following the choral reading, students are divided into groups of two or three and are given about five minutes to continue practicing the text with their partners. One student reads the passage while the partners follow along silently and provide help as needed as well as positive and formative feedback. Each student in a group practices in this manner.

6. At this point, students are usually able to read the text with some degree of fluency. In order to make the FDL an authentic and artful activity, students are then invited to perform their text for an audience. The audience can simply be other classmates, but it can also consist of volunteer adults stationed outside the classroom or even other classrooms of students.

7. Word Work. At the end of the performance, the teacher and students select five to ten words from the passage and engage in a quick and intensive word study. Study activities can include finding other words that contain a selected rhyme or word family from the passage (for example, from the poem *Rain, Rain, Go Away!*, other *ay* words such as *day, play, stay,* and *stray* can be discovered and

displayed for students to read), sorting the set of selected words in various ways, examining the morphological nature of certain words (for example, *bi-* is a morpheme in *bicycle* and *biplane* that means two; other words that contain the *bi-* morpheme and that refer to two include *bifocals, biannual, biceps,* and so on), and playing word games such as WORDO! and Word Ladders.

8. Repeated Reading at Home. The FDL continues at home as students take their second copy of the passage and are encouraged to read and perform the passage to family members at home a number of times, usually five or more readings. Family members are encouraged to listen to the student's reading and provide praise and encouragement for the student's efforts and accomplishments.

9. Repeated Reading. Ideally, a new FDL is implemented the following day with a new text. However, before beginning to read the new text, the teacher leads students in reading and celebrating their mastery of texts from previous days. If the FDL cannot be implemented daily, we recommend that a lesson be done a minimum of three times per week, as one lesson provides reinforcement to the next.

The key elements required in any FDL are modeling fluent reading, assisted reading, repeated reading, and word work implemented within the scope of one lesson – thus synergy. The essential goal for any FDL is for students to achieve success with a new text (poem) with each lesson in terms of word recognition accuracy, automaticity, expression, and confidence. A number of research studies have demonstrated the efficacy of the FDL in improving not only fluency and word recognition, but also comprehension and overall reading achievement (DiSalle & Rasinski, 2017; Zimmerman et al., 2019; Zimmerman, Rasinski, & Melewski, 2013).

Another example of synergistic instruction was developed in response to a struggling third grade reader. The intervention was called Read Two Impress (Young, Rasinski, & Mohr, 2016). The student was reading at a first grade level and was referred to the reading specialist for specialized instruction. Because he was a dysfluent reader, the reading specialist decided to use repeated readings. The student made some good gains in reading automaticity, but he rarely read with expression. So, the reading specialist thought using the neurological impress method might help with his expression. However, because repeated readings were also working so well, the reading specialist wanted to continue. So, the interventions were stacked and worked synergistically to improve the student's reading. After about 18 weeks, the student was reading on grade level. Further research on Read Two Impress suggested that it is a viable option for reading intervention (Young, Pearce, et al., 2018). Here are the steps used in Read Two Impress:

1. Choose a text that is challenging for the student.
2. Make sure you and the student have a copy of the text.
3. Read a page or paragraph aloud together.
4. Read slightly ahead of the student.
5. Read with good expression that matches the meaning of the text.
6. Have the student reread the page/paragraph aloud.
7. Continue with subsequent page/paragraphs for 20 minutes.

Making Fluency Instruction Artful

So, the science of reading tells us that reading fluency is important for developing proficiency in reading. The science of reading also provides tools or guideposts for developing fluency instruction. Is it possible to use these tools in artful ways in order to make fluency instruction engaging, creative, and authentic for students? Of course, the answer is yes.

One of the scientific cornerstones of fluency instruction is repeated reading where a student reads a text orally multiple times until that reading begins to approach the level of fluency exhibited by a more proficient reader. Another, and perhaps more common or authentic, name for repeated reading is "rehearsal." When rehearsing a script in a play or a poem for performance at a poetry slam, the person doing the rehearsing is reading the text multiple times to achieve an appropriately expressive oral reading, not a fast reading. This is an authentic use of repeated readings.

Thus, regularly performing (and rehearsing) a script, poem, song, monologue, speech, or other text meant to be performed for an audience is an artful approach to nurturing fluency in students. Readers' Theater, by the way, which we mentioned previously, is one form of script reading that is particularly useful for classroom use. In Readers' Theater performances, there is usually no actual acting (movement), costumes, props, scenery, or memorization involved. Performers simply stand or sit in front of an audience and read their parts. However, since there are none of those other accoutrements, which can make putting on a play an enormous task in a school setting, performers must perfect their oral reading in order to provide the audience with a satisfying performance.

This notion of rehearsal and performance is the key to artful fluency instruction. Making a performance a weekly activity (usually happening at the end of the week) will make fluency instruction a central part of the classroom literacy curriculum. Here's how a rehearsal and performance protocol might work: Every Monday morning, the teacher assigns students texts that will be performed at the end of the week. These could be, for example, scripts, poems by a particular poet, or seasonal songs. Texts can be assigned to individuals, pairs, small groups, and even the whole class. Then, throughout the week, students spend 10 to 20 minutes per day in rehearsal. Rehearsal at home is also a great way to make a home connection. Early in the week, the rehearsal can take the form of the teacher reading the texts to students while students follow along silently. Later, the rehearsal can include various forms of choral reading, and still later, students can rehearse with partners or in small groups with some students listening and providing formative feedback. By Friday, students are ready to perform for an audience. The audience can just be the class members themselves but may also include other guests such as invited family members, the school principal, and other available school personnel. The performance can even be video recorded for publication on the school or classroom website. The following Monday, the routine begins again with new texts to be performed on the next Friday.

One of the interesting and artful evolutions of this approach to fluency instruction is that students begin to consider and actually create their own performance materials and develop their own performances (Young & Rasinski, 2011). Students may write their own poems based on poems and poets they have performed in the past, songs that are parodies of other popular tunes, and even short scripts that are developed from texts or excerpts of texts students may be reading in other areas of the literacy curriculum. The performances can go beyond live classroom events to actual movies that are scripted, rehearsed, and performed by students (Young & Rasinski, 2013). What began as a fluency protocol can evolve into a writing curriculum in which students use mentor texts to develop their own writing and express meaning. Authentic and artful instruction has a way of expanding well beyond its original instructional intent.

Of course, the key scientific question for such instruction is: "Does it actually work to improve students' reading fluency and other reading outcomes?" A number of studies as well as reviews of research have demonstrated the positive effects of artful fluency instruction in a number of different instructional contexts and with students at a variety of grade and reading achievement levels (Martinez, Roser, & Strecker, 1999; Griffith & Rasinski; Rasinski et al., 2011; Young & Rasinski, 2018; Young, Durham, Miller, Rasinski, & Lane, F., 2019). Thus, we can say that such instruction is both scientific and artful.

Achieving reading fluency is essential for achieving proficiency in reading, and because reading is so critical for all learning, fluency is essential for students' academic learning and lifelong reading. When we can use the scientific essentials for fluency and find ways to teach them in ways that are also artful, we are more likely to move students well beyond improving their performance on fluency assessments to finding new ways to make reading engaging and meaningful.

References

Allington, R. L., & McGill-Franzen, A. M. (2021). Reading volume and reading achievement: A review of recent research. *Read Res Q*, 1–8. https://doi.org/10.1002/rrq.404

DiSalle, K., & Rasinski, T. (2017). Impact of short-term fluency instruction on students' reading achievement: A classroom-based, teacher initiated research study. *Journal of Teacher Action Research*, 3, 1–14. Retrieved from www.practicalteacherresearch.com/uploads/5/6/2/4/56249715/impact_of_short-term_intense_fluency_instruction_.pdf

LaBerge, D., & Samuels, J. (1974). Toward a theory of automatic information processing in reading. *Cognitive Psychology*, 6, 293–323.

McKenzie, S. C., McGhee, J., & Reid, C. A. (2019). National Assessment of Educational Progress (NAEP) results: 2019. *Policy Briefs*. Retrieved from https://scholarworks.uark.edu/oepbrief/150

Paige, D. D., Magpuri-Lavell, T., Rasinski, T. V., & Smith, G. (2013). Interpreting the relationships among prosody, automaticity, accuracy, and silent reading comprehension in secondary students. *Journal of Literacy Research, 46*(2), 123–156.

Paige, D. D., Rasinski, T. V., & Magpuri-Lavell, T. (2012*).* Is fluent, expressive reading important for high school readers? *Journal of Adolescent & Adult Literacy, 56*(1), 67–76.

Rasinski, T. V. (1990). *The effects of cued phrase boundaries in texts.* Bloomington, IN: ERIC Clearinghouse on Reading and Communication Skills (ED 313 689).

Rasinski, T. V. (2010). *The fluent reader: Oral and silent reading strategies for building word recognition, fluency, and comprehension* (2nd ed.). New York: Scholastic.

Rasinski, T. V., Padak, N. D., Linek, W. L., & Sturtevant, E. (1994). Effects of fluency development on urban second-grade readers. *Journal of Educational Research, 87,* 158–165.

Rasinski, T. V., Padak, N., McKeon, C., Krug-Wilfong, L., Friedauer, J., & Heim, P. (2005). Is reading fluency a key for successful high school reading? *Journal of Adolescent and Adult Literacy, 49,* 22–27.

Rasinski, T. V., Reutzel, C. R., Chard, D., & Linan-Thompson, S. (2011). Reading fluency. In M. L. Kamil, P. D. Pearson, B. Moje, & P. Afflerbach (Eds.), *Handbook of reading research* (Vol. IV, pp. 286–319). New York: Routledge.

Samuels, S. J. (1979). The method of repeated readings. *The Reading Teacher, 32,* 403–408.

Schreiber, P. A. (1980). On the Acquisition of Reading Fluency. *Journal of Reading Behavior, 12*(3), 177–186. https://doi.org/10.1080/10862968009547369

Valencia, S. W., & Buly, M. R. (2004). Behind test scores: What struggling readers really need. *The Reading Teacher, 57*(6), 520–531.

Young, C. J., Durham, P., Miller, M., Rasinski, T., & Lane, F. (2019). Improving reading comprehension with readers theater. *Journal of Educational Research, 112*(5), 615–626. doi:10.1080/00220671.2019.1649240

Young, C. J., Pearce, D., Gomez, J., Christensen, R., Pletcher, B., & Fleming, K. (2018). Examining the effects of read two impress and the neurological impress method. *Journal of Educational Research, 111*(6), 657–665.

Young, C. J., & Rasinski, T. V. (2011). Enhancing author's voice through scripting. *The Reading Teacher, 65*(1), 24–28.

Young, C. J., & Rasinski, T. V. (2013). Student-produced movies as a medium for literacy development. *The Reading Teacher, 66*(8), 670–675.

Young, C. J., & Rasinski, T. V. (2018). Readers theatre: Effects on word recognition automaticity and reading prosody. *Journal of Research in Reading, 41*, 475–485.

Young, C. J., Rasinski, T. V., & Mohr, K. A. J. (2016). Read two impress: An intervention for disfluent readers. *Reading Teacher, 69*(6), 633–636.

Zimmerman, B. S., Rasinski, T. V., Kruse, S. D., Was, C. A., Rawson, K. A., Dunlosky, J., & Nikbakht, E. (2019). Enhancing outcomes for struggling readers: Empirical analysis of the fluency development lesson. *Reading Psychology, 40*(1), 70–94. doi:10.1080/02702711.2018.1555365

Zimmerman, B. S., Rasinski, T. V., & Melewski, M. (2013). When kids can't read, what a focus on fluency can do. In E. Ortlieb & E. Cheek (Eds.), *Advanced literacy practices: From the clinic to the classroom* (pp. 137–160). Bingley, UK: Emerald Group Publishing. https://doi.org/10.1108/S2048-0458(2013)0000002010

6 | Artful Teaching of Vocabulary

Mr. White teaches fifth grade and was preparing a social studies lesson on vegetation. As he read through the text, he immediately recognized that students would not understand the meaning of content-specific words such as *biome* and *prairie*. As he prepared his lesson, Mr. White also wondered if all students would understand several of the "non-disciplinary" words such as *transform*, *precede*, and *evolve*. "Would comprehension suffer if students did not know the meaning of just a few words, and are some more critical than others?" He also wondered, "What does this mean for my instruction?" This question is in the middle of the intersection where artful teaching and reading science meet. A group of researchers investigated this very question. After studying hundreds of students from eight countries, they found that there is no free pass when it comes to understanding words as every unknown word means less understanding of a text (Schmitt, Jiang, & Grabe, 2011). The researchers also found no vocabulary "threshold" where knowing most of the words meant it was unnecessary to know the rest of the words. While understanding every word does not guarantee full comprehension, the authors found that if an aspirational goal for readers is 60 percent comprehension, then knowledge of 98 percent of the words is necessary. As Mr. White continued his lesson preparation, he wondered how he would know which words students knew, which they didn't, and how he would teach word meanings and still have time for the lesson content. As he thought, it occurred to him that because knowing the meaning of words is so important to comprehension, in a very real way, teaching the meaning of words *is* part of teaching the content.

DOI: 10.4324/9781003218609-6

Teaching vocabulary is an authentic teaching challenge that all teachers grapple with. In this chapter, we begin with a review of the science about vocabulary. We then turn our attention to several strategies that can artfully help students better understand the meanings of words.

The Role of Vocabulary

Vocabulary is critical to understanding text, whether narrative or disciplinary (Joshi, 2005; Joshi & Aaron, 2000; Zywica & Gomez, 2008). Research shows that by the end of second grade, the lowest quarter of students know about 4,000 words, the average student knows about 6,000 words, and the top quarter of students know 8,000 words (Biemiller, 2005). Considering these large differences, it is reasonable to wonder how vocabulary knowledge develops. The answer begins with the quantity and quality of household language exposure in the first years of a child's life (Hart & Risley, 1995; Huttenlocher, Vasilyeva, Waterfall, Vevea, & Hedges, 2007; Hirsh-Pasek et al., 2015; Rodriguez & Tamis-LeMonda, 2011; Rowe, 2012). This is why, as teachers, we see such differences among students in the words they bring to the classroom. Evidence also suggests that the age at which a child is exposed to literacy is related to vocabulary knowledge some ten years later (Sun et al., 2020). By the time children are in first grade, their vocabulary knowledge predicts their reading comprehension in eleventh grade (Cunningham & Stanovich, 1997). In multiple studies, vocabulary knowledge has been repeatedly found to influence a reader's ability to comprehend text (Anderson & Freebody, 1981; Hock et al., 2009; Paige, Rasinski, & Magpuri-Lavell, 2012; Seifert & Espin, 2012; Stahl, 1990). By the time students reach early adolescence, vocabulary knowledge has become indistinguishable from reading comprehension (Ricketts, Lervåg, Dawson, Taylor, & Hulme, 2020).

New Word Acquisition

As they progress through school, students are acquiring new words at an astounding rate. Estimates are that students acquire approximately 2,500 to 3,000 new words per year, culminating in a reading vocabulary estimated at about 25,000 words by the end of elementary school and 50,000 by the end of high school (Anderson & Nagy, 1992). While vocabulary knowledge influences comprehension of story text (Biemiller, 2010), Lee and Spratley (2010) contend that it is essential to understanding the particular concepts found in content texts, what they refer to as "disciplinary literacy" (p. 2). Nagy and Townsend (2012) explain that content texts contain academic language used by experts to discuss their discipline. These texts are characterized by abstract words, syntax, and ideas that are often compressed into dense sentences. So, Mr. White is correct. Teaching the meaning of words is a critical piece of teaching the content.

Students learn vocabulary in a variety of ways, including from direct instruction (Nation, 2001), through discussion (Stahl & Vancil, 1986), and through extensive reading (Elley, 1991; Nation, 2001). While Nagy (1995) contends that routine teaching of vocabulary is not generally an efficient use of instructional time, the results of meta-studies (an analysis of multiple studies) disagree with results showing large effects for word meanings that were taught directly to students (Stahl & Fairbanks, 1986). For the vocabulary found in disciplinary literacy texts, Beck, McKeown, and Kucan (2002) suggest that content-specific words must be taught explicitly if students are to acquire their meanings and develop command of the language. Vocabulary size appears to also make a difference in writing quality. For example, in an elementary study, students with deeper knowledge of science and social studies vocabulary were found to be better at disciplinary-specific argumentative writing (Kim, Relyea, Burkhauser, Scherer, & Rich, 2021). Scammacca and Stillman (2018) studied eighth grade social studies students and found that vocabulary predicted both content acquisition and reading comprehension. While reading is one way to learn new words, Swanborn and de Glopper (1999) found that eleventh grade students had only a 33 percent chance of learning word meanings while reading. These authors argue, as have Shany and Biemiller (2010) with third and fourth grade readers, that students lack the necessary strategies to learn new word meanings from text and require direct word instruction.

Word Tiers

In his book *Words Worth Teaching* (2010), Biemiller explains that children acquire word meanings in a known sequence. Words learned by the primary grades are those heard in the home environment which most children are exposed to. Biemiller and Slonim (2001) found that average first and second grade students know about 2,500 words, what are called Tier 1 words. Tier 2 words are those that more advanced students know by the end of second grade, while Tier 3 words are those specific to content areas and are best learned in those classes. Biemiller recommends teaching words known by 40 percent to 80 percent of students by the end of second grade. Words known by fewer than 40 percent of students are unlikely to be learned during the primary grades, while words known by more than 80 percent of students are likely to be learned without instruction. The word list identified by Biemiller contains about 1,600 words and breaks down to about 500 new words per year across first through third grades. Helping students acquire these word meanings would narrow the vocabulary gap among students.

A cautionary note is in order regarding the productivity of learning words when reading – what is known as learning from context. We cited research showing that readers have about a one in three chance of learning a word while reading. This raised the question of when context is helpful. Consider the following sentence: *The crew was not certain if the cable would bear the load.* In this case, context tells the reader that the word *bear* is likely not referring the big furry critter with long claws and sharp teeth. For context to work in this case, the reader must have knowledge of the word meaning as it's used in the sentence – to hold weight. Although learning the meaning of new words from context is often promoted as effective, reading research has not always supported this, particularly for low-vocabulary students (Beck et al., 2002; Schatz & Baldwin, 1986; Stahl, 1999). You may be wondering how this can be. While some early research did find context clues to be productive, many of these studies used words within tightly controlled and predictive sentences that greatly improved the chance of successfully using context. Take, for example, this cloze sentence where the student is asked to use context to choose from among three words: *The old/cranky/pretty lady was the star of the show.* Of the three choices, *pretty* might be an obvious answer. Two other examples: *The day was cold as _____. He drank a cup of _____ coffee.* Here, *ice* and *black* fit nicely. Now, consider this sentence: *He took the envelope with an enigmatic smile.* If the reader does not know the word *enigmatic,* the interpretation that the smile was mysterious would be difficult to make. This is a case where sentence context is of little help in understanding the word. Schatz and Baldwin (1986) conducted three experiments with tenth and eleventh grade students and found that context had no statistically significant effect on the ability to learn words. Unfortunately, classrooms across the country ring out with teachers encouraging students to *use your context clues*. A knowledgeable teacher understands when context can be helpful for learning new words and when it is not.

With an understanding that vocabulary learning requires direct instruction, what are effective methods for teaching vocabulary? Let's explore several that are supported by research and artfully fit with authentic instruction.

Artful Teaching

As we mentioned earlier, artfully teaching vocabulary is sometimes perceived as a tug-of-war with teaching the content. But it doesn't have to be. New words can certainly be taught directly by telling students the meaning that reflects the context in which they're being used in the text. While this solves the immediate problem, we also know that students are likely to quickly forget the meaning or not understand it sufficiently. The challenge becomes how to help students transfer the word so it becomes part of their vocabulary.

As we discussed earlier, many words have more than one meaning with connotations based on the context in which they're used. As students become more familiar with words, they are regularly adding these connotations to their word knowledge – in other words, they are increasing their *depth* of knowledge about individual words. The artful teacher understands that word connotations add to the student's schema (background knowledge) about the topic within which the word is used. To help build schema through vocabulary, artful teachers can help students make these words "sticky" – that is, help students remember word meanings. Making a word sticky requires that students use the word multiple times in various modes. This is where artful teaching comes in. We'll now review several ways of learning new words. These include word ladders, word maps, using a dictionary, concept picture sorts, and the Four Es.

Word Ladders

Word ladders are visual aids that help students enhance their understanding of words by learning the subtleties in meaning between words. By learning how words are related, students are also building their schema, or background knowledge, about a topic. There are various applications of word ladders, and we'll look at two of these.

The first begins by selecting two opposite, target words that you want to teach. Once the target words have been decided, select several words that are related to the two target words. In our example, we've selected *day* and *night* as the target words, along with four other, related words (*sunrise, dawn, twilight,* and *dusk*) for a total of six words. As you can imagine, we're not so interested in teaching *day* and *night,* as students know those words. We are simply using *day* and *night* as bookends to help students learn the other four words. Begin the lesson by telling the class they are going to "learn more about two words, *day* and *night,* and four other related words." Having decided on a total of six words, we now know that our word ladder needs six rungs. On the board or overhead, draw a ladder with six rungs. Now, write the two target words on the bottom and top rungs of the ladder. It would be helpful for students to draw a word ladder in their journals and fill in the words as you make them available. Next, ask the students to write a short definition for *day* and *night* in their journals. When they are finished, have a brief conversation about the definitions to arrive at a common understanding. Remember that your definitions of *day* and *night* should be developmentally appropriate based on the grade and depth of understanding of your students. Also, if the content you are teaching has specific meanings, you will want to introduce those. Return to the word ladder and write *sunrise* under *day*. Ask for a volunteer to explain *sunrise*. Then explain that *sunrise* is the point when the edge of the sun is first visible on the horizon. It is likely that students may not know what *horizon* means, so this may have to be explained also. A picture like the one here

Earth's horizon

Figure 6.1 Earth's horizon.

can help students grasp the concept. *Horizon* can be explained to children as the point where the sky appears to meet the earth. It helps to see the horizon if one is in the country and away from buildings and trees that can obscure the view. By the way, with our use of *horizon* in the explanation of *sunrise*, we've come across a great example of how words are related to deepen schema about a topic. The next word on the ladder is *dawn*, the point before sunrise when there is light in the sky but the sun is not yet visible. Have students write *dawn* in their word ladder and then ask who knows what it means. Finish the activity with the words *twilight* and *dusk*.

Similar to the activity described in the phonics chapter, Rasinski (2005) offers another version of this called vocabulary ladders. Each ladder is composed of ten words with a clue provided for each word. Vocabulary ladders turn the word ladder into a kind of detective activity. Unlike the previous example, the words are not part of a conceptual word family. For example, the ladder begins with a word that is provided for the student. A clue is then provided to help the student identify the second word. The clue tells the student how to manipulate the first word (change or add a letter) to arrive at the second word. In this way, students climb their way up the vocabulary ladder by identifying words at each rung until they've reached the top. More advanced ladders may ask the student to delete or rearrange the letters to arrive at the next word. As the words are not conceptually related to each other, this approach creatively builds word flexibility and thinking in the student – and it's fun.

From these two examples, you can see how word and vocabulary ladders can be used to teach important vocabulary from an upcoming reading, build general vocabulary knowledge, and engage students in generative thinking about words. Ladders provide authentic engagement with words

---

day
sunrise
dawn
twlight
dusk
night

Figure 6.2 Word ladder.

and cause students to purposively think about how they are related. Word and vocabulary ladders are flexible and can be applied to general word learning and to content-specific words.

Morphology – A Root Awakening

In phonics, we often talk about sound units of language. When talking about building vocabulary, there is another unit of language that we should attend to: morphemes and morphology. A morpheme is a language unit that bears meaning. The most common morphemes we teach are prefixes and suffixes. Children learn early on how prefixes such as *re-*, *pre-*, *un-*, and *dis-* and suffixes such as *-ing*, *-or*, and *-tion* alter the meaning and grammatical category of words. But there is so much more that we can do with morphemes or what we like to call "word roots." We call them word roots because from one word root can emerge many branches or English words. Some of the most common and useful word roots come to us from Latin and Greek. It has been estimated that well over half of multisyllabic words as well as academic or disciplinary words are derived at least in part from Latin and Greek word roots (Rasinski, Padak, Newton, & Newton, 2020). Take, for example, the Latin root *terr/ter*, which means "earth" or "land." Knowing this one morpheme, students can get at the very least a toehold on words such as *territory, terrain, terrace, extraterrestrial, Mediterranean, terrarium*, and many more.

The easiest way to teach word roots is simply making students aware of essential morphemes, their meanings, and words that belong to the word root family. Five to ten minutes two to three times per week devoted to making students aware of word roots can go a long way to building students' vocabularies. Each week, put a word root on display on a "Word Wall" and display English words that belong to that word root family. Below, we present a beginning list of word roots that you may wish to teach your students. See for yourself – what English words contain these roots and how is the meaning of the roots embedded in these words?

Common Word Root Bases

aero(o)   air, wind

audi, audit   hear, listen

bibli(o)	book
bio	live, life
chron(o)	time
dem	people
graph, gram	write, draw
hydr(o)	water
labor	work
mand	order
mater	mother
max	greatest
pater	father
phil/phile	love
phon	voice, call sound
photo	light
pod	foot
pol, polis	city
port	carry
scop	look, watch
stru, struct	build
terr, ter	land, ground, earth

Common Word Root Prefixes

ante	before
anti, ant	against, opposite
auto	self
bit	wo
co, con	with, together
ex	out
mega, megalo	big
micro	small
multi	many (Latin)

poly	many (Greek)
pre	before
re	back, again
super, sur	on top of, over, above
tele	far, from afar
tri	three
un	not
uni	one

Below are two examples of Word Walls using word roots.

Bi- = Two/2
Bicycle
Bicuspids
Biceps
Bifocals
Biplane
Binoculars
Biannual
Bipartisan
Bilingual
Bicameral
Biped
Bisect
Bipolar

Terr/Ter = Earth
Terrace
Terrain
Territory
Terrier
Terracotta
Subterranean
Extraterrestrial
Mediterranean
Interment

Imagine the interesting discussions you might have with students as you challenge them to figure out the meaning to words that can be on the surface quite challenging.

Be Creative – Be the Bard

One of the principles we have noted of artful reading instruction is giving ourselves and our students license to be creative. Word root study allows you and your students to be, much like William Shakespeare, creators of new words. Besides writing his poems, sonnets, and plays, Shakespeare invented words. Nearly 10 percent of all the words he used were of his own creation – *courtship*, *excitement*, *premeditated*, *green-eyed*, *skim milk*. It's not hard to notice that what Shakespeare often did was to combine existing word roots. Well, if he can do it, why not challenge students to "be like the bard" and invent their own words? Indeed, they can. Here are two words that were invented by intermediate grade students we have worked with. Can you figure out their meanings? (Answers are at the end of this chapter.)

Autophile   Matermand

Students love the challenge of inventing words and then stumping their classmates (and teacher) in trying to determine the meaning of their word inventions. When we allow students to be artful and creative in this way, they are certain to anchor their understanding of essential word roots and the English words that belong to the word root families.

Word Maps

The artful teacher understands the power of visuals in helping students learn a concept. A word map is another visual aid that helps students develop a concrete idea of what a word really means (Schwartz & Raphael, 1985). A word map uses three categories of relationships to help the student learn a word and is particularly applicable to nouns. Three questions about these categories are asked about the word: 1) what is it? 2) what is it like? and 3) what are some examples? A word map is similar to another strategy called the Frayer model, with the difference being it does not ask the student to draw a pictorial representation of the word (Frayer, Frederick, & Klausmeier, 1969). A word map begins by placing the target word in a box. Above the box, the question "What is it" is answered. In our example below, the word *catamaran* is the target word and it is defined as a boat. To the right, "What is it like" provides several specific features of a catamaran. A catamaran has two hulls, sometimes three; the hulls are parallel to each other, meaning they sit side-by-side in the water; and the cabin part of the boat sits on top of the hulls. The last part of the word map provides several examples of a catamaran. Catamarans can be sailboats, they can be built to ferry cars, they can be quite large like a ship, and they can be pleasure yachts with motors. A good practice when introducing a word map is to use overhead or whiteboard technology to include the visual so that all students can see the map as it's built. Once students understand how to construct a map, they can be provided paper templates to construct their own map. Experience with word maps helps students learn what defines a word. This becomes important when students use a dictionary, our next word learning strategy.

A goal of vocabulary instruction is to help students become independent word learners. Dictionaries have been used by generations of students to learn words. Prior to digital technology, many of us kept a dictionary at home as a quick reference to learn unknown words encountered in readings and assignments (yes, Tim still has his from college). With the advance of Internet technology, it is now easy to look up word meanings using online dictionaries. However, we will learn that students have

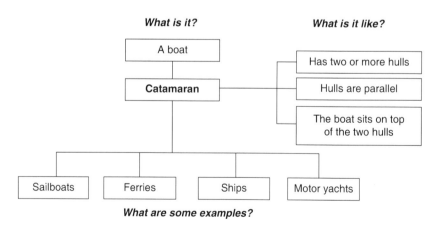

Figure 6.3 Dictionaries.

considerable difficulty using and applying the information they find in dictionaries. Research on dictionary use is filled with nuance and complexity. An understanding of what students gain from dictionaries can help artful teachers as they instruct students in how to use a dictionary.

To begin, researchers offer three big guidelines regarding word learning. First and fundamentally, frequent exposure to word definitions is beneficial to students (McKeown, Beck, Omanson, & People, 1985). Teaching students new word *definitions* improves word knowledge but not necessarily comprehension. Second, the more encounters a student has with a word, the better their knowledge of the word. Third, rich instruction extending beyond the classroom is necessary for children to acquire a larger and better integrated schema for associated words. These findings help the artful teacher match their goal for vocabulary instruction with the outcomes they can expect from students. For example, do not expect students to "know" a word simply by looking up its definition in the dictionary. However, learning how to use a dictionary to increase exposure to word definitions is helpful, while at the same time it's important to know the challenges that students face when using a dictionary.

Scott and Nagy (1997) provided additional insight into the difficulty in helping students deepen their word knowledge. The authors found that students have fundamental problems understanding new word definitions obtained from a dictionary. On first blush, one may think, well, of course, definitions can be obtuse and difficult to understand. To further delve into this issue, Scott and Nagy rewrote definitions for simplicity and put them into grade-appropriate language. They found that whether a definition was straight out of the dictionary or written for simplicity, the result was the same. Students tended to take a fragment of a definition and ignore the rest of the information. Even when given high-quality, contextual examples of the word along with simplified definitions, students showed significant inattention to the sentence structure of definitions that resulted in considerable difficulty correctly applying the word in context. Because they often have only partial knowledge of the word, students are likely to incorrectly apply it in context. This is why a teacher may see a sentence turned in by a student reading "I *belated* my mother's birthday." The authors concluded that integrating dictionary information into a contextual sentence is a much more complex task for students than what teachers presume.

Given the background on the challenges with teaching the meanings of words, dictionaries are, in fact, a rich source of word knowledge that when used correctly, quickly provide information about words. As teachers, it is helpful to be aware that learning a word meaning and then correctly applying it in writing is a complex process for students. This is not to discount the usefulness of dictionary definitions. Rather, it is helpful to be aware that while dictionaries are a rich source of word knowledge, they present challenges for students. In fact, it is likely that any teaching of word definitions may result in only a partial understanding by students and require additional instruction and scaffolding.

Continuing on, sorting is a strategy that people have been using for millennia and one that artful teachers can adopt to teach a variety of different concepts. Sorts have been used in hundreds of creative ways – for example, helping young children learn shapes by sorting wooden blocks. Biologists, on the other hand, catalogue the complexity found in plants and animals into countless categories that can be sorted. Sorting is an authentic human activity that be adapted to artful vocabulary teaching.

Concept Picture Sort

Let's consider an example of sorting for kindergarten children that teaches both knowledge of words and concepts. Tell the class that they are going to help you sort a set of animal pictures into two groups, one that lives in water and one on land. For this activity, you gather pictures of a dog, lion, bird, fish, whale, snake, shark, dolphin, and frog. On the bulletin board, you make a "T" that gives you two sides to display the pictures. You label one side of the "T" *land* and the other side *water*. To begin the lesson, tell the students, "I'm going to show you some pictures of animals, but I need your help. Tell me whether the animal lives in water or on land. I will then put the picture in the correct category of the board." Show the class the picture of a shark and ask, "Where does a shark live, on land or in the water?" After students have told you "in the water," display the picture on the board under the water column. Continue this procedure for the rest of the pictures, saving the frog for last. Now ask the children, "Where does a frog live?" There may be a discussion, with some replying on land and others in the water. Explain that frogs spend their early life in the water as tadpoles and later on land as frogs who also go into the water. Frogs belong to a third category of animals called amphibians. "We will need to make another category on the board for frogs," you explain. "We'll label it amphibians." This is a simple example of a picture sort using pictures of authentic animals. Another, more creative sort for older children would be to gather a collection of words (no pictures) and sort them based on two, simultaneous characteristics. Before beginning the sort, students need to know the meaning of each word. For example, consider the words *pharmacy, jumping, chills, hospital, throw, clinic, nurse, doctor, pediatrician, fever, limping, running, dehydrated, sprint, gridiron, sick, bed, ball,* and *error.* Ask the students to sort the words based on these characteristics:

1. Multisyllabic and medical
2. Single syllable and sports
3. Multisyllabic and sports
4. Single syllable and medical

Tell the students to make a chart like the one below and to then label the four categories as we have in the example below. Next, model how to sort the first word for two, simultaneous categories. Ask the class whether the word *nurse* is a single syllable or multisyllabic and why. Next, ask if the word is more readily associated with the medical field or with sports. *Nurse* is both single syllable and associated with medicine, so it goes in the single syllable row under the medical column. Tell the students to use this procedure to sort the remaining words into one of four categories.

This type of sort encourages critical thinking about the meaning of words based on their content (medical or sports) and syllabic characteristics (single or multiple). There are many other, creative ways to construct word sorts that encourage word knowledge and critical thinking in students.

	Content	
Syllables	Medical	Sports
Single syllable	Nurse, bed, sick, chills	Spring, ball, throw, sprint
Multisyllabic	Pharmacy, hospital, clinic, doctor, pediatrician, fever, limping, dehydrated	Jumping, running, gridiron, error

When Context Is Helpful

Earlier, we mentioned some of the challenges in learning a word from context. However, artful teachers can help students become word sleuths by paying close attention to clues provided by the author. The creative teacher will explain how clues to the meaning of a word may appear in or around a word. Let's revisit Mr. White and his lesson on the prairie. He had identified five words that he thought he should teach his students: *transform*, *precede*, *prairie*, *evolve*, and *biome*. Mr. White decided he would create an artful activity to help students learn when context can help them learn word meanings. He focused on five different kinds of context clues often given by authors and then created sentences that highlighted each one.

1. *Providing an appositive definition*: Sometimes, authors will use a word and then elaborate in such a way that the meaning becomes apparent. They haven't given a definition, but the careful reader will figure out the word. For the word *transform*, Mr. White wrote the following sentence:

   > In the springtime, just a little rain will *transform* a desert, changing it from a landscape with dry and dull vegetation to one teeming with green plants and colorful flowers.

From this sentence, the reader can infer that *transform* refers to a change.

2. *Showing when the author has given an example*: Mr. White showed students with this sentence that while an author may not, again, directly define a word, an example might be provided:

   > Oftentimes in nature, one event *precedes* another, such as when hot, humid weather leads to a thunderstorm.

This sentence mentions two events: hot, humid weather and a thunderstorm. The two are linked in such a way that explains what the word *precedes* means: to come before.

3. *Providing an antonym*: A sentence may be crafted where the use of a word is followed by its opposite meaning, thus providing a clue to the meaning of the first word.

> While adequate rain and sunshine help young forests *evolve* into mature stands of trees, a forest fire may *stop* the entire process, leaving nothing but charred trunks.

In this sentence, the reader may wonder about the meaning of *evolve*. Later in the sentence, the word *stop* is used that links back to *evolve*. The careful reader can infer that in this sentence, *evolve* refers to the *growth* of trees, which was stopped by the fire.

4. *Giving a helpful synonym*: This is similar to the previous example, except that now the helpful word is a synonym.

> As we drove across the *prairie*, we were amazed at the tranquil beauty of the unending pastures.

If the reader is unfamiliar with the word *prairie*, the end word *pastures* gives a clue to its meaning.

5. *Pointing to a general clue*: In this example, the word's meaning must be inferred from the text and may involve several sentences to become known. In this case, the reader is not familiar with the word *biome*.

> *Biomes* across the earth demonstrate the diversity of the planet. One particular *biome* is characterized by fresh water such lakes, ponds, and streams that are surrounded by land. Another kind of *biome* features large open ranges covered with tall, wild grasses and few trees. Forests are a kind of *biome* that feature dense growths of trees that are home to many species of birds, mammals, and insects.

From these four sentences, it becomes clear that *biome* refers to the various features that make up a particular habitat. It is also clear that there can be various kinds of biomes.

For each of his five examples, Mr. White could ask his students to determine what the target word means. Following that, he could have students identify how the author is helping the reader with the meaning of the italicized word. Rather than simply telling students the various ways in which authors provide word clues, Mr. White creatively engages students in an inductive process where they must analyze what the author is doing in each sentence and how it helps illustrate the meaning of the word. By creating this discovery process, students are much more likely to remember to look for clues provided by the author to unlock word meanings.

We now turn our attention to several principles for vocabulary teaching and to a vocabulary teaching procedure called the Four Es.

Foundational Principles

Now that we've reviewed several artful strategies for vocabulary teaching, we can now identify four anchor principles to keep in mind when teaching vocabulary.

1. When teaching a definition, put it into context. Let students know that context is important and that the meaning of a word is often dependent on its context (remember the *bear* example).

2. To learn words, students must be cognitively engaged. This means they need to discuss examples, respond to questions, use the new word in speech, and engage in other kinds of activities requiring processing of the word.

3. Teach relationships between words. Our earlier word ladder example is one way to do this, while a word map is another. Learning words requires that students become aware of the nuances among words, and we've identified several excellent ways that the artful teacher can encourage that learning.

4. Students must have multiple exposures to a new word, and they must transfer it to their spoken and written vocabulary. Students need to hear teachers use words in context and they should be corrected when they misunderstand or misuse words. Teachers should also take opportunities to point out the relationships among words.

The Four Es

At the beginning of the chapter, Mr. White was considering how to help his students learn new words. The Four Es is a procedure for teaching words. The e's stand for *explain*, *engage*, *extend*, and *examine* (Watts-Taffe,

Gwinn, & Forrest, 2019). Let's help Mr. White become an even more artful teacher by applying the Four Es.

Explain: Mr. White can begin by introducing a new word and explaining it using a student-friendly definition. Let's use our earlier word *prairie*. After introducing the word, Mr. White puts the word on the whiteboard so that everyone can see it and then has them read the word aloud. All students must be looking at the word while saying it several times to give their orthographic processors opportunity to transfer the word to their lexical memory. Mr. White explains to his fifth graders that a prairie is a large area of land in the middle of America that is flat and covered with tall grasses. At this point, he could show them pictures of a prairie. He could display a map and point to the areas of the country where prairies are found. Mr. White could create a word ladder to help teach the word.

Engage: It's now time for students to become actively engaged with the word. Mr. White could ask if any students have ever seen a prairie. Do they know anyone who lives in the states where prairies are found? He could then put two or three questions on the whiteboard for students to discuss with each other. For example, what kind of plants and animals live on a prairie? Do students know that millions of American bison once roamed the prairies?

Extend: To help students remember the word *prairie* and its meaning, Mr. White can give students several opportunities over the course of a week to speak and write the word. Mr. White should use the word frequently when speaking to students and expect them to use the word.

Examine: Mr. White can take note of the extent to which students are using *prairie* correctly and incorporating it into their writing and speaking. Do students use the word appropriately? Are they comfortable when using it in conversation? Do students appear to recognize the word in formative assessments? By taking note of how students are using the word, Mr. White is able to reteach and make corrections to shape the correct use of the word among his students.

Making It Artful, Authentic, and Creative

Effective teaching is about shaping young minds into critical, curious, and creative thinkers. To do this well requires capturing the imagination of students – certainly not an easy task! Vocabulary undergirds much of what it means to be an educated person. As teachers in today's standards-driven environment, we often struggle with the demands of covering the content versus encouraging deep understanding in students. Knowing the meanings of words and developing the skill to effectively use them in speaking and writing is critical to both learning and academic success. It is important that as teachers, we use our creativity to develop artful and authentic ways to teach vocabulary every day. Students need all the vocabulary they can learn, as evidence suggests that even among college students, vocabulary knowledge is less than that required to effectively understand college-level texts (Treffers-Dalle & Milton, 2013). We hope that you will continue to grow your ability to artfully teach students the power of words.

- "Be the Bard" words invented by students:

  Autophile (auto = self; phile = love): Someone who is in love with themselves – a narcissist
  Matermand (mater = mother; mand = order): A mother's order.

References

Anderson, R. C., & Freebody, P. (1981). Vocabulary knowledge. In J. Guthrie (Ed.), *Comprehension and teaching: Research reviews* (pp. 77–117). Newark, DE: International Reading Association.

Anderson, R. C., & Nagy, W. E. (1992). The vocabulary conundrum. *American Educator*, *16*(14–18), 44–47.

Beck, I. L., McKeown, M. G., & Kucan, L. (2002). *Bringing words to life: Robust vocabulary instruction*. New York: Guilford Press.

Biemiller, A. (2005). Size and sequence in vocabulary development: Implications for choosing words for primary grade vocabulary instruction. In E. H. Hiebert & M. Kamil (Eds.), *Teaching and learning vocabulary: Bringing research to practice* (223–242). Mahwah, NJ: Erlbaum.

Biemiller, A. (2010). *Words worth teaching: Closing the vocabulary gap.* Columbus, OH: McGraw Hill SRA.

Biemiller, A., & Slonim, N. (2001). Estimating root word vocabulary growth in normative and advantaged populations: Evidence for a common sequence of vocabulary acquisition. *Journal of Educational Psychology, 93*(3), 498–520. https://psycnet.apa.org/doi/10.1037/0022-0663.93.3.498

Cunningham, A. E., & Stanovich, K. E. (1997). Early reading acquisition and its relation to reading experience and ability 10 years later. *Developmental Psychology, 33*(6), 934–945.

Elley, W. B. (1991). Acquiring literacy in a second language in a second language: The effect of book-based programs. *Language Learning, 41,* 375–411.

Frayer, D., Frederick, W., & Klausmeier, H. (1969). *A schema for testing the level of cognitive mastery*. Madison, WI: Wisconsin Center for Education Research.

Hart, B., & Risley, T. R. (1995). *Meaningful differences in the everyday experience of young American children*. Brooks: Baltimore.

Hirsh-Pasek, K., Adamson, L. B., Bakeman, R., Owen, M. T., Golinkoff, R. M., Pace, A., . . . Suma, K. (2015). The contribution of early communication quality to low-income children's language success. *Psychological Science, 26*(7), 1071–1083. doi:10.1177/0956797615581493

Hock, M. F., Brasseur, I. F., Deshler, D. D., Catts, H. W., Marquis, J. G., +Mark, C. A., et al. (2009). What is the reading component skill profile of adolescent struggling readers in urban schools? *Learning Disability Quarterly, 32*(1), 21–38.

Huttenlocher, J., Vasilyeva, M., Waterfall, H. R., Vevea, J. L., & Hedges, L. V. (2007). The varieties of speech to young children. *Developmental Psychology, 43,* 1062–1083. https://psycnet.apa.org/doi/10.1037/0012-1649.43.5.1062

Joshi, M. R. (2005). Vocabulary: A Critical Component of Comprehension, *Reading and Writing Quarterly, 21*(3), 209–219. https://doi.org/10.1080/10573560590949278

Joshi, R. M., & Aaron, P. G. (2000). The component model of reading: Simple view of reading made a little more complex. *Reading Psychology, 21*(2), 85–97. https://doi.org/10.1080/02702710050084428

Kim, J. S., Relyea, J. E., Burkhauser, M. A., Scherer, E., & Rich, P. (2021). Improving elementary grade students' science and social studies vocabulary knowledge depth, reading comprehension, and argumentative writing: A conceptual replication. *Educational Psychology Review*. https://doi.org/10.1007/s10648-021-09609-6

Lee, C. D., & Spratley, A. (2010). *Reading in the disciplines: The challenges of adolescent literacy*. New York: Carnegie Corporation of New York.

McKeown, M. G., Beck, I. I., Omanson, R. C., & People, M. T. (1985). Some effects of the nature and frequency of vocabulary instruction on the knowledge and use of words. *Reading Research Quarterly, 20*(5), 522–535. https://doi.org/10.2307/747940

Nagy, W. E. (1995). *Technical report no. 627: On the role of context in first- and second- language learning*. University of Illinois Urbana-Champaign: Center for the Study of Reading. Retrieved from www.ideals.illinois.edu/handle/2142/31277

Nagy, W. E., & Townsend, D. (2012). Words as tools: Learning academic vocabulary as language acquisition. *Reading Research Quarterly, 47*, 91–108. doi:10.1002/RRQ.011

Nation, I. S. P. (2001). *Learning vocabulary in another language*. Cambridge: Cambridge University Press.

Paige, D.D., Rasinski, T.V., & Magpuri-Lavell, T. (2012). Is fluent, expressive reading important for high school readers? Journal of Adolescent & Adult Literacy, 56(1), 67–76. doi:10.1002/JAAL.00103

Rasinski, T. V. (2005). *Daily word ladders: 100 reproducible word study lesson that help kids boost reading, vocabulary, spelling & phonics skills – independently*. Grades 2–3. New York: Scholastic.

Rasinski, T. V., Padak, N., Newton, R., & Newton, E. (2020). *Building vocabulary with Greek and Latin roots* (2nd ed.). Huntington Beach, CA: Shell Educational Publishing.

Ricketts, J., Lervåg, A., Dawson, N., Taylor, L. A., & Hulme, C. (2020). Reading and oral vocabulary development in early adolescence. *Scientific Studies of Reading, 24*(5), 380–396. https://doi.org/10.1080/10888438.2019.1689244

Rodriguez, E. T., & Tamis-LeMonda, C. S. (2011). Trajectories of the home learning environment across the first 5 years: Associations with children's vocabulary and literacy skills at prekindergarten. *Child Development, 82*(4), 1058–1075. https://doi.org/10.1111/j.1467-8624.2011.01614.x

Rowe, M. L. (2012). A longitudinal investigation of the role of quantity and quality of child-directed speech in vocabulary development. *Child Development, 83*(5), 1762–1774. https://doi.org/10.1111/j.1467-8624.2012.01805.x

Scammacca, N., & Stillman, S. J. (2018). The effect of a social-studies based reading intervention on the academic vocabulary knowledge of below-average readers. *Reading and Writing Quarterly, 34*(4), 322–337. https://doi.org/10.1080/10573569.2018.1446855

Schatz, E. R., & Baldwin, R. S. (1986). Context clues are unreliable predictors of word meaning. *Reading Research Quarterly, 21*, 439–453. https://doi.org/10.2307/747615

Schmitt, N., Jiang, X., & Grabe, W. (2011). The percentage of words known in a text and reading comprehension. *The Modern Language Journal, 95*(1), 26–43. https://doi.org/10.1111/j.1540-4781.2011.01146.x

Schwartz, R. M., & Raphael, T. E. (1985). Concept of definition: A key to improving students' vocabulary. *Reading Teacher, 39*(2), 198–203. Retrieved from www.jstor.org/stable/20199044

Scott, J. A., & Nagy, W. E. (1997). Understanding the definitions of unfamiliar verbs. *Reading Research Quarterly, 32*(2), 184–200. https://doi.org/10.1598/RRQ.32.2.4

Seifert, K., & Espin, C. (2012). Improving reading of science text for secondary students with learning disabilities: Effects of text reading, vocabulary learning, and combined instruction. *Learning Disabilities Quarterly, 35*(4), 236–247.

Shany, M., & Biemiller, A. (2010). Individual differences in reading comprehension gains from assisted reading practice: Pre-existing conditions, vocabulary acquisition, and amounts of practice. *Reading and Writing, 23*(9), 1071–1083. doi:10.1007/s11145-009-9196-4

Stahl, S. A. (1990). *Beyond the instrumentalist hypothesis: Some relationships between word meanings and comprehension.* Technical Report No. 505 of the Center for the Study of Reading, University of Illinois at Urbana-Champaign.

Stahl, S. A. (1999). *Vocabulary development.* Cambridge, MA: Brookline Books.

Stahl, S. A., & Fairbanks, M. M. (1986). The effects of vocabulary instruction: A model-based meta-analysis. *Review of Educational Research, 56*(1), 72–110.

Stahl, S. A., & Vancil, S. J. (1986). Discussion is what makes semantic maps work in vocabulary instruction. *The Reading Teacher, 40*, 62–67.

Sun, M., de Schotten, M. T., Zhao, J., Song, S., Zhou, W., Gong, G., . . . Shu, H. (2020). Influences of the early family environment and long-term vocabulary development on the structure of white matter pathways: A longitudinal investigation. *Developmental Cognitive Neuroscience, 42*, 100767. https://doi.org/10.1016/j.dcn.2020.100767

Swanborn, M. S. L., & de Glopper, K. (1999). Incidental word learning while reading: A meta- analysis. *Review of Educational Research, 69*(3), 261–285. doi:10.3102/00346543069003261

Treffers-Daller, J., & Milton, J. (2013). Vocabulary size revisited: The link between vocabulary size and academic achievement. *Applied Linguistics Review, 4*(1), 151–172. https://doi.org/10.1515/applirev-2013- 0007

Watts-Taffe, S., Gwinn, C. B., & Forrest, C. (2019). Explain, engage, extend, examine: Four E's of vocabulary instruction. *Texas Journal of Literacy Education, 7*(1), 25–43.

Zywica, J., & Gomez, K. (2008). Annotating to support learning in the content areas: Teaching and learning science. *Journal of Adult and Adolescent Literacy, 52*(2), 155–165. https://doi.org/10.1598/JAAL.52.2.6

Artful Teaching of Comprehension*

After having read the short story "Pappa's Parrot" from Cynthia Rylant's book *Every Living Thing* (1985), instead of asking students a list of prepared questions that were his typical approach to fostering reading comprehension in students, fourth year teacher Tom Sutten decided to try a new "artful" approach he had read about in one of his graduate courses on reading education. The approach was called "tableau" and involved individual students or small groups of students choosing a scene from the story and creating a "still life" or "living picture" using their bodies as the paints for their paintings. In groups of three and four, students scattered to different parts of the classroom to choose the scene they wished to depict.

"I was stunned by the conversation the students were having. They never talked this much about any story we had read. First, they got into animated discussion of which scene to choose, then they argued over who would play who, and finally they worked with one another to place themselves and determine an appropriate statuesque gesture or position to provide visual clues for the audience of their classmates." After a quick ten minutes of discussion and work, Mr. Sutten called time and asked students to return to their seats. Then, one group after another came to the front of the class and arranged themselves. Mr. Sutten then did a countdown: "Three, two, one . . . freeze." At the word "freeze," students were to freeze in place and make the gestures they had determined in their planning. As each group stood in their statuary position, the rest of the class had to determine what scene was being portrayed by each tableau. While most of the scenes were highly predictable, class members in the audience engaged in

---

* This chapter is created with contributions by William D. Nichols.

DOI: 10.4324/9781003218609-7

examining each tableau for clues as to the actual scene. Once a consensus was reached, each tableau group was released from their freeze and engaged in a discussion on why and how they chose their scene.

"I had never heard the term 'tableau' used before," Mr. Sutten said. "But I can tell you this: I will be using it again and again. The level of enthusiasm and engagement by students was remarkable. More importantly, if comprehension is the process of evaluating and constructing meaning, that is what my students were doing – creating meaning, and then inviting their classmates to make inference about the meaning (scenes) they had made."

Defining Reading Comprehension

So, what do you think it means when we say someone comprehends a text? Most would reply that someone comprehends a text if the person understands what is happening in the text and can recall details from the text. However, does that answer completely explain reading comprehension? What do we mean by "understand," and how do we provide evidence of understanding?

Perhaps your previous experiences in an elementary classroom make you think comprehension of text focuses on the learner's ability to retell the events in the text in chronological order. Many teachers listen to students read in guided reading or whole class settings and attempt to measure learners' comprehension of the text by asking students to recall the details of the text so the teacher can assess a reader's comprehension. The student is believed to comprehend the text if they are able to recall the majority of the details in a text and can retell the details in the order they occurred in the story or text. Other teachers may measure comprehension based on the connections that students make to the text, focusing on text-to-self, text-to-text, and text-to-world connections.

Reading comprehension and reading comprehension instruction may be among the most challenging reading competencies to wrap our heads around. Without doubt, comprehension is a reading competency validated by science (National Institute of Child Health and Human Development, 2000). Common sense tells us that it is the ultimate goal of the reading act. Yet, when most people are asked to define "comprehension," they often respond with "understanding what is read." Then, when asked about "understanding," they often go back to "comprehending what is read." While not denying the key element of "understanding what is read" as a part of comprehension, we don't find it helpful in deepening our own understanding of the concept and how it may be nurtured instructionally in artful teaching.

How do we know when we understand something that is read? In many classrooms (and test situations), comprehension, or understanding, occurs when a reader is able to answer correctly questions about the text just read. From an artful and authentic perspective, we do not see this as a very satisfying indication of comprehension. How often do we as adult proficient readers read a text for the purpose of answering questions that are posed to us about the text? Not often, we suppose.

Perhaps a more authentic way of looking at how comprehension takes place happens when we examine our purpose and what we do with a text after we read and comprehend it. The short answer is "we do something" with what we read. In our own professional lives, we write as part of our duties. If you look at just about any professional article or book that we have written (including this one), you will find a list of references – other books and articles that we read and consulted in preparing our own piece of writing. We had to read and comprehend the texts that are referenced in order to produce our own writing. "Doing something" (our own writing) provided us with a reason for our own reading and comprehending. We feel that an artful approach to reading comprehension first looks at an authentic reason for reading. Once a real reason is established, the various techniques or methods for engaging in comprehension can become part of our instructional milieu.

Why do we read? Why do our students read? Of course, there are many reasons for this. Renowned literacy scholar P. David Pearson (2021) says that we read for three primary purposes: knowledge, insight, and inspiration. We might add a fourth reason: for entertainment/enjoyment. We learn to learn something new just as we have in our professional careers and perhaps for the very reason you are reading this book. We read to gain insight into things – perhaps to examine how others feel about a particular political or social issue. We read to be inspired. How many of us have read a poem, story, or other such text and had that aesthetic response – perhaps goose bumps, perhaps tears. Certainly, we had to understand the text, at least in our own personal way, to respond with goose bumps or tears. Even though we have read them multiple times, it is difficult for us to read the first lines by Emma Lazarus on the side of the Statue of Liberty ("Give me your tired, your poor, your huddled masses yearning to breathe free") or the last lines of the Gettysburg Address ("government of the people, by the people, for the people, shall not perish from the earth") without getting a lump in our collective throats. And, of course, we read for the pleasure of it – to enjoy a good story. When we start with a reason for reading, we lay the foundation for comprehension.

How to "Do Something" with What We Read

One of the best ways to conceptualize "doing something" with texts is through the lens of Project/Problem Based Learning (PBL). The notion of PBL goes back to the days of John Dewey and the progressive era in education. In PBL, students identify a project they wish to pursue (under the guidance of the teacher). The project could be developing a brochure about the local community; becoming advocates for a local environmental cause; determining how children, families, and teachers feel about some issue such as recess or school libraries; developing a history of their school; or producing a poetry slam or Readers' Theater presentation around some topic of interest or inspiration. In order to engage in such projects successfully, students will have to gain information about their topic. This can be gleaned through various multimedia sources, through conversations and interviews with others, and also through reading related texts. When reading has a purpose, students have a need and desire to comprehend – to gain knowledge and insight. Pearson (2021) argues that reading, as well as writing and language, should be viewed as tools to gain knowledge, insight, and inspiration (and to that we also add pleasure or enjoyment). He further argues that when students are able to apply their ideas from reading and other sources, they are demonstrating the highest form of comprehension.

Most of us remember Bloom's taxonomy of learning from an early psychology course we may have taken in college. The taxonomy was a way to conceptualize various levels of learning, or in regard to reading – comprehension. A more recent version of the taxonomy is now available

(Anderson et al., 2001; Krathwohl, 2002). At the lowest levels of learning/comprehension, we see remembering and understanding. Certainly, these can be considered part of comprehension. That is why teachers often ask students to recall what they have read as a way to nurture and assess comprehension. But this is low-level comprehension. To allow our students to grow in comprehension, we should be challenging them to engage in higher levels of comprehension and learning. In Bloom's new taxonomy, the highest level of learning is "create." When you can take what you have learned or comprehended from a text and use that knowledge to make something new, you are demonstrating the highest form of comprehension. Keep in mind that one of the key characteristics of artful reading instruction is that it is creative. Thus, by aiming reading comprehension to creative ends, we are providing instruction that not only has a scholarly/scientific basis, but also a footing in art.

Are approaches to comprehension that challenge students to be creative – to put what they have read and learned to work to make something or solve a problem – effective? A recent large-scale scientific study of PBL examined the impact of four social studies projects (units) on the educational achievement of second grade students (Duke, Halvorsen, Strachan, Kim, & Konstantopoulos, 2021). Results found that the PBL group showed higher growth in social studies and informational reading over a group of students who received more traditional instruction in social studies.

Projects and Problems – Big and Small

So, perhaps an artful way to think of reading comprehension is to start not with skills or strategies for comprehending texts, but to consider authentic projects that students can engage in and complete and problems they can solve that will require them to read and comprehend. Let's consider just a few.

In Chase Young's second grade class, the students were challenged by their teacher to "put on a show" for parents and other audience members. So, after reading a trade book story such as *The Polar Express* (Van Alsburg), the students worked to transform the story into a script that could then be rehearsed and performed for the classroom's family holiday get-together.

The focus was not initially on comprehension but fluency. Basing the project on a book that the students had already read and comprehended put the focus not on comprehension but on rehearsing (repeated reading) and performing. Indeed, this was a great activity for fluency, but what Chase also found was that as his students were developing their scripts, they had to dig more deeply into the original text than they had before – examining the text for character traits, motivations, even the creation of possible props to use in the performance. Students had to add narration and character dialogue to carry the story from book form to stage. Later, Chase noted that in adding narration and creating dialogue, students were actually making inferences about the story. Inferential comprehension is universally considered one of the highest forms of comprehension. "What a revelation," Chase said. "What started as a fun activity for improving fluency (which it did) turned out to be a great approach for improving students' comprehension. The discussion that students engaged in when developing their scripts was so high level."

Turns out that any sort of transformation of one text into another form can set the stage for significant comprehension building. When students transform a story into script, an informational piece into a persuasive essay, a short poem into a story, they will be required to comprehend the original text in a much deeper way than simply reading the text as an assignment. Students could be challenged in other ways to "transform" a text. Perhaps they could be asked to consider and write a prequel to the story they have just read or look into the future and develop a sequel and write what will happen next.

Even the vignette that began this chapter described a form of transformative project. Students took scenes from a story they had read and transformed them into a series of still life representations using their bodies as the building blocks for their representations. Similarly, students could transform a text into a number of other forms and formats – a traditional illustration, a digital illustration, a comic strip, a mime, and so on. What other forms of transformations and representations can you think of?

Projects and problems can take students outside the classroom. In the report we cited earlier (Duke & Halvorsen, 2017), students visited a local park and noted problems and deficiencies in their visit. From this, students read and studied more deeply how the problems could be solved, developed a plan, and presented the plan to the local government.

Consider the meaningful and motivated reading that students engaged in when involved in this project. They read material that may have been well above their own reading levels. Yet, the desire to accomplish motivated and inspired them to read, understand, and "do something." (As we noted earlier, the report indicated that project-based learning, of which this particular project was a part, resulted in higher gains in social studies learning and reading proficiency than a more traditional approach to teaching social studies.)

In another project, middle grade students were involved in a project to bring companionship and comfort to residents of a nursing home near the middle school. In the project, students were partnered with a nursing home resident and met with them once or twice a week. One of the tasks within the larger project was for the students to take oral histories of their partners. In the process of doing so, the students engaged in a fairly intensive study of aging. They attended presentations by experts in aging, and they also read and gave their own reports on material read. In the process of developing, talking, and writing the oral histories of their partners, students learned from their partners about growing up in a time before the students themselves were born. The highlight of the project was a ceremony in which the students presented written copies of their oral histories to their partners. Not only did students comprehend and learn about the nature of aging in general, they also developed deep relationships with their nursing home partners. Students not only experienced cognitive growth, but also through the aesthetic nature of the project showed emotional and empathetic growth as well.

Many of us belong to book clubs where we get together with friends and acquaintances to read and discuss our take on books or other texts that we read in common. We are part of such clubs for a number of reasons – we want to do something with the books we read: enjoy a book with others, share our understandings and insights and hear the understanding of others about stories we read together, develop and nurture friendships, be part of a larger community with common interests. Students have similar needs themselves. Creating book clubs or discussion groups is a project for which students have the same intentions. The object of such discussions is not a teacher-led quiz to assess recall, but an attempt to create the same authentic and aesthetic experiences we have as adults when we engage in book or text discussions and debates.

Comprehension Strategies and Instruction that Fit into the Artful Project

The projects we describe above are just a sampling of the many types of projects that students, under the guidance and support of a teacher, can engage in. In this next section, we explore how the various comprehension strategies that have been endorsed by science and scholarly opinion can be woven into the fabric of the projects.

Background Knowledge

Have you ever tried reading a text for which you have little background knowledge? Usually, your comprehension is difficult and limited for such texts. We often find this happening when our undergraduate students take their first reading education course. Initially, their knowledge of the topic and vocabulary is limited. However, as they attend class and continue with their reading, their comprehension and ease of reading improves considerably. Their increasing knowledge on the topic facilitates their comprehension. Whether you call it schema, background knowledge, or simply knowledge, it has been well established that to be able to comprehend a text well, you need to have some knowledge of the content in advance of reading. In the pre-learning phase, the objective is to assess, build, and activate student background knowledge, set a purpose for learning, and motivate the learners to want to engage in the theme or project.

Background knowledge is even more important for our younger readers, as by their very nature of being children, their knowledge is limited. As teachers, we need to help students develop their knowledge for whatever project or reading they will be undertaking. How can this be done?

Perhaps the best way to build background knowledge for future reading and learning is to read to students related material. This can be related books, segments from books, picture books (even for older students), articles from newspapers, and social media (as long as you can verify its veracity). You can also bring in speakers who have some degree of background and expertise in the knowledge you wish to build in students. And, of course, other media such as films and videos (such as from YouTube) offer a great way to introduce students to a topic.

Hypothesizing and Predicting

We think of reading and learning to read as a science as well as an art. What is at the heart of the scientific method? Hypothesis or prediction! Scientists often will state a hypothesis or prediction about a particular phenomenon and then engage in scientific inquiry to determine whether the hypothesis is true or not.

We look at readers as engaging in scientific inquiry. You may not realize this, but if you are a proficient reader, you are constantly hypothesizing. You are just so good at it that you may not realize it. Have you ever read a book or a chapter of a book and been surprised by the ending? Of course. We all have. Having been surprised is evidence that you made a prediction – "I made a prediction; it didn't come true; I'm surprised."

Challenging students to make predictions or hypotheses when reading is a powerful way to engage them in making meaning. Moreover, there are many ways that you can encourage predictions. One of the easiest ways is to allow students to make predictions after seeing the title to a text or a short introduction to it. In such instances, students will need to rely on their background knowledge as well as the limited information from the introduction to make reasonable predictions. Once the predictions are made, students then engage in reading to confirm or disconfirm their predictions. Then, at various stopping points throughout the text, students can be allowed to analyze their predictions and make revisions based on new information that has been read.

Another approach to predictions is an activity we call "prevoke," or predictions based on vocabulary. Simply put, you provide students with a selection of key words from a text they are about to read, present them in the order in which they will appear in the text, ensure that those students have some degree of understanding of the vocabulary, and then invite them to offer predictions about the text they will be reading. Once the reading has been completed, students can discuss the text vis-à-vis their predictions. How were their predictions in line with the passage and how did they diverge? Students love the idea of attempting to figure out puzzles. In this case, the puzzle is the text they are about to read.

Text Talk

Earlier, we mentioned how text discussion groups can be a project in and of itself. However, discussion can and should be used within all forms of reading and projects. As students progress through schooling, they tend to either find themselves barely speaking in small-group discussions or attempting to speak over classmates and making little progress. In order to create new understandings that are co-constructed by classmates, teachers must gradually scaffold information through the power of meaningful discussion and text talks (Gilles & Pierce, 2020). Allowing students to use their own talk and expanding their perspectives allows teachers to investigate different lines of thinking with their classes and can help build background and a consensus of understanding. Additionally, when encouraging students to engage in discussion, teachers need to create a safe environment where learners are encouraged to explore new and challenging ideas (Gilles & Pierce, 2020). In order for students to feel secure in sharing their knowledge and insights, students need to understand, recognize, and value diverse perspectives and navigate differences that lead to a thorough understanding. This is what helps students challenge their preconceived notions from both fiction and nonfiction texts alike.

Like bundling background and predictions, discussions related to reading can take a variety of forms. Discussion can be among pairs of students or larger groups. Students can be assigned specific roles in a discussion. Discussions can center around a specific set of questions posed by the teacher or students. However, one form of discussion that should be avoided is the traditional classroom discussion in which the teacher asks primarily literal questions of specific students in the class for the purpose of checking students' recall or remembering of the text. That form of discussion is neither authentic, creative, or artful. In all types of discussions, the aim should be for students to share their own creative insights from the reading.

Writing

Note-taking is an activity any serious investigator uses in learning about a topic. Certainly, all of us know of a reporter's notebook. Asking students to keep notes as they read and learn about a particular topic not only provides them with documentary evidence of their learning, but also provides them with the grist necessary for discussion and further writing on the topic. A great way to help students engage in note-taking is to model the process for them as we read informational and narrative texts to them, and then to talk about the process we went through and the decisions we made in taking notes.

Similarly, having students write in a reading response journal encourages thoughtful analysis and understanding of texts they read. There is something quite powerful about writing – it slows down our thinking and makes us more reflective on what we have read and learned. Regular entries in response journals can take a variety of forms, from specific prompts given by the teacher to more open-ended writings in which students are free to write about whatever may have struck them in their reading.

Visualization

Have you ever seen a movie based on a book you previously read? If so, is the movie ever as good as the book? Most often, the answer is "no." The reason why the book is usually better than the movie is that you have already seen the book in your head as you read the book. The movie version of the book is somebody else's version – and of course your version matches the way you see the text playing out. Visualization is an authentic activity that proficient readers engage in often. Scientific research has found visualization to be a powerful tool for promoting comprehension. When students create a mental image of a text being read, they are pulling information from their background knowledge and combining it with the text in order to create their own representation (or meaningful image of the text). We would prefer to enlarge the notion of visualization to include not just what is seen, but also what may be heard, what may be felt, what may be smelled or tasted, and even what might be felt emotionally.

A great way to promote visualization or imagery is simply to ask students to draw their representations on paper as they read a text and then share their images with other members of their group. In their sharing, students will focus on what they considered important aspects of the reading and also bring other sensory and emotional details that are part of the image. Visualization could easily fit into larger discussions of the text.

Compare and Contrast

Compare and contrast is a meaning-making activity that we engage in frequently as adult readers and learners. We do so when we are shopping for household appliances, when we make predictions about how well our sports teams may do this season, or when we decide which candidate for political office we will support and vote for. In that process, we read relevant materials about these topics, juxtapose them against one another, compare and contrast, and come to a final conclusion or determination.

Compare and contrast is a powerful tool for learning and comprehending, and engaging students in the making of good comparisons and contrasts is well worth the effort. In reading, we often create such situations by asking students to compare something they have read, or some element of what they have read with something else – a previous text that was read, a current event, perhaps even comparing a character from a story with themselves or other characters. In project-based learning, compare and contrast can play an important role. In projects, students are often tasked with making decisions that require compare and contrast – comparing one course of action with another, one policy with another, and so on. A key to effective compare and contrast is to determine key points or characteristics against which students will do their compare-contrast analysis. Simple language can often set the stage for comparing and contrasting (and can easily fit within discussion groups or note-taking):

•   How is this story like the one we read earlier? What is similar, and what is different?

•   How are the events portrayed in this text like what recently happened in the world?

- What are the pros and cons of one decision versus another course of action?

When engaging in such analyses, readers are required to read a text closely and with the aim of extracting important information.

Sometimes, we come across actual trade books that can promote certain reading competencies. One of our favorites is *I Am the Dog, I Am the Cat* by Donald Hall (1994). Initially, we saw this as a great way to promote fluency. The book is written as parallel monologues with a dog and cat who live in the same household. The book is written in script form, so two students can pair up, rehearse, and perform the book for an audience. Great fun!

However, it didn't take long to notice that *I Am the Dog, I Am the Cat* is also a book that involves comparing and contrasting – how the dog and cat see the same world in which they live. With that in mind, the book took on the nature of a project as we have challenged students to write their own versions of the book that involve comparing and contrasting. Here are just some titles our students have written:

I Am a Lizard, I Am a Frog

I Am an Octopus, I Am a Gila Monster

I Am Ohio, I Am Pennsylvania

I Am a Democrat, I Am a Republican

I Am a Deciduous Tree, I Am a Coniferous Tree

Just about anything you would want students to compare and contrast can be written about and comprehended using *I Am the Dog, I Am the Cat* as a mentor text and mini-project.

Rehearsal and performance were mentioned in our earlier chapter on fluency. However, rehearsal (repeated reading) followed by performance is also a good way to promote comprehension. We often call this form of rehearsal "close reading," as students are asked to read a text more than once for different purposes. Knowing that students will be asked to perform a particular text will require them to consider the conveyance of meaning in their performances. They may have to experiment with how they use their voices to make a satisfying and meaningful performance. Moreover, when students do perform their assigned text for an audience, the audience members themselves will have an opportunity to learn (comprehend) the information that the performers have themselves learned.

Of course, to get the biggest impact for any comprehension strategy, it should be implemented within the context of a meaningful and authentic project. Additionally, the strategies should be implemented in combination with one another. When students use discussion, note-taking, and visualization within one reading, they are creating synergy where one strategy amplifies the effectiveness of the others. Indeed, using multiple strategies within the context of an authentic project will itself create a synergy in which the project itself creates a meaningful motivator to come to a full understanding of the texts read.

Don't Forget the Foundations

Now that we have shared with you the way we think about comprehension and comprehension instruction as an art, we want to be sure to emphasize that we not forget the scientific foundations of reading. If comprehension is the point of reading, then it must sit on a strong foundation. In reading, that foundation includes print knowledge, phonemic awareness, phonics or word decoding, vocabulary, and reading fluency – both automaticity in word recognition and prosody. Readers cannot understand a text for which they cannot decode or understand the words or for which they are unable to read fluently. We have addressed each of these areas in previous chapters of this book. The essential takeaway from these chapters is that when you teach phonics, vocabulary, or fluency, you are also teaching comprehension. Making meaning should always be part of any artful reading instruction.

Last Word

Comprehension may be a rather straightforward topic. Comprehension instruction, however, is a bit more complicated. Comprehension instruction is not simply teaching students a set of strategies that they employ when reading. Rather, we feel that comprehension instruction should begin with a reason for reading – a project, if you will, that students and teacher wish to accomplish. When we begin with an authentic purpose, we open up the way for students to use those strategies to not only comprehend and learn from texts, but also as an accomplishment for which students can take justifiable pride. And when you think about it, isn't that what reading, and all learning, is all about?

References

Anderson, L. W. (Ed.), Krathwohl, D. R. (Ed.), Airasian, P. W., Cruikshank, K. A., Mayer, R. E., Pintrich, P. R., . . . Wittrock, M. C. (2001). *A taxonomy for learning, teaching, and assessing: A revision of Bloom's taxonomy of educational objectives* (Complete ed.). New York: Longman.

Duke, N. K., & Halvorsen, A. L. (2017, June 20). *New study shows the impact of PBL on student achievement.* Edutopia. George Lucas Foundation. Retrieved from www.edutopia.org/article/new-study-shows-impact-pbl-student-achievement-nell-duke-anne-lise-halvorsen

Duke, N. K., Halvorsen, A. L., Strachan, S. L., Kim, J., & Konstantopoulos, S. (2021). Putting PjBL to the test: The impact of project-based learning on second graders' social studies and literacy learning and motivation in low-SES school settings. *American Educational Research Journal, 58*(1), 160–200. https://doi.org/10.3102/0002831220929638

Gilles, C., & Mitchell Pierce, K. (2020). Talking about books: Scaffolding deep discussions. *The Reading Teacher, 74*(4), 385–393. https://ila-onlinelibrary-wiley-com.wv-o-ursus-proxy02.ursus.maine.edu/doi/10.1002/trtr.1957

Hall, D. (1994). *I am the dog; I am the cat.* New York: Dial Press.

Krathwohl, D. (2002). A revision of Bloom's taxonomy: An overview. *Theory into Practice, 41*(4), 212–218. doi:10.1207/s15430421tip4104_2

National Institute of Child Health and Human Development. (2000). *Report of the national reading panel, teaching children to read: An evidence-based assessment of the scientific research literature on reading and its implications for reading instruction* (NIH publication no. 00-4769). Washington, DC: U.S. Government Printing Office.

Pearson, P. D. (2021, September 14). A conversation with P. David Pearson. *Classroom Caffeine Podcast*. Season 2, Episode 9. Retrieved from www.classroomcaffeine.com/guests/david-pearson

Rylant, C. (1985). *Every living thing*. New York: Atheneum/Richard Jackson Books.

8 Artful Assessment of Reading

Mr. Parsons:	sat down with one of his third graders, Archer, who was reading a book about cats.
Mr. Parsons:	Why did you choose this book, Archer?
Archer:	I like cats and I want to know everything about them.
Mr. Parsons:	Can you understand the book okay?
Archer:	Most of it.
Mr. Parsons:	What parts do you find challenging?
Archer:	There are some words that I have never heard before.
Mr. Parsons:	How are you dealing with those words when you get to them?
Archer:	I look in the glossary, but sometimes they are not there, so I just keep reading.

Mr. Parsons has artfully assessed Archer's reading comprehension through an authentic conversation about the book. Reading researchers agree that measuring reading comprehension directly can be challenging, but in this case, Mr. Parsons did exactly that – he asked Archer whether he could understand what he was reading. In doing so, Mr. Parsons and Archer were able to identify vocabulary as a source of misunderstanding. Indeed, Mr. Parsons could have asked Archer to state the main idea and three supporting details or ask Archer explicit questions about the content of the text. However, none of these approaches to assessment would have revealed so

DOI: 10.4324/9781003218609-8

quickly that vocabulary was the culprit. The teacher empowered the student to self-report their level of understanding, and together they realized the issue. Of course, the conversation you read above is not groundbreaking, but sometimes in the face of science, we can overlook more simple and authentic ways to assess a student's reading proficiency.

A Brief History

In 1918, Edward Thorndike began to conceptualize reading assessments based on the notion that reading was reasoning. Thus, there was something going on inside the mind of a reader, and he posed that if we could begin to isolate those processes, we could effectively assess reading proficiency. Based on this, early assessments primarily assessed reading comprehension and proficiency through short-answer questions. During the 1930s, we see the emergence of multiple-choice assessments. After World War II, the essay became a popular means for assessing reading. By the 1970s, we saw a plethora of ways to assess reading that ranged from informal to standardized assessments. We believe that these more recent developments in formative assessment were helpful for teachers when planning instruction based on the results.

Reading Is Developmental

Some of the key developments in reading assessments were based on the belief that reading was developmental and students passed through certain stages. One of the most popular models of reading development comes from Chall's (1996) Stages of Reading Development. Chall proposed six stages, starting with stage zero: 0) Prereading, 1) Initial Reading and Decoding, 2) Confirmation and Fluency, 3) Reading for the Learning of the New, 4) Multiple Viewpoints, and 5) Construction and Reconstruction. Indeed, the stages sound rather sophisticated, but we will break them down for you and show how they relate to assessment and instruction. However, stages four and five are beyond the scope of this book, but are worth mentioning so we can keep the end goal in mind. Although students do not pass through these stages at the same time, and there are certainly deviations, viewing reading as developmental can inform our assessment practices and corresponding instruction. The art of assessment begins with selecting the appropriate assessments for your individual students. In the following section, we show examples of assessments that might be suitable for students in particular stages.

Reading Assessment Through the Stages

Prereading

In this stage, typically from birth to around age six, children begin to play with language, which later serves as a foundation for reading development. Related to reading, children begin to understand what reading might be. Concretely, children begin to recognize a book and its features. There are some concepts about print that young children need to learn in order to merge into the stage. Indeed, we say "merge" because it is not a distinct ascension from one stage to another – there is a great deal of overlap, and transition duration and age vary. So, do not expect your students to automatically hit stage one on their sixth birthday.

Some concepts about print that children acquire in the prereading stage include recognizing a book, identifying the front and back covers as well as information those typically contain (such as title, author, illustrator), how to hold a book correctly (not upside down or backward), and how to open a book. It may seem intuitive to you, but we are not born knowing these concepts; they have to be learned. Once the book is open, we also want to make sure that children understand the concepts found in a book, such as knowing what letters and words are – not necessarily being able to read them, but able to say, "Hey, these are letters and these are words." All of these concepts are crucial to learn for emergent readers.

There are a host of assessments available that assess reading readiness, which is essentially what the prereading stage is mostly about. Typically, these assessments test a student's concepts about print. Usually, you will choose an easy book, sit with your student one-on-one, and assess what they know about books. We have provided an example below (Figure 8.1).

Prompt	Correct? ✔ / X
Place a book on the desk or table and use the prompts with your student.	
Concepts of a Book What is this on the table?	
What do you do with it?	
Please point to the front cover.	
Please point to the title.	
Please point to the author.	
Please point to the illustrator.	
Where is the back cover of this book?	
Pick up the book and open it.	
Where should I start reading?	
Concepts of Print Please point to any letter.	
Please point to any word.	
Please point to the first letter in this word.	
How many letters do you see in this word?	
Do you see any capital letters?	
How many words are on this page?	
Do you see any punctuation? (Define or give examples if necessary.)	

Figure 8.1 Example concepts about print assessment.

Of course, there is another way to informally assess a student's concepts about print, which is more artful. What we are about to propose is groundbreaking, and it is meant only for your ears. Ready? You can ask them to read with you. Not in a teacher/student assessment kind of way, but in a "let's read a book together for fun and we like each other" kind of way. During that time, when you are bonding over a book, you can observe the child's "reading" behaviors. You are likely able to determine if child knows what a book is, understands how it works, and recognizes some important features. In this approach, you not only show that reading can be a fun social experience, but you also get a decent idea of the child's concepts about print. This approach is more authentic because you are engaging in a real reading experience. It can also be more aesthetic, because you are not sitting at the teacher table in assessment mode. Instead, you might be relaxing on a big beanbag (aka lice transmitter) in the reading corner, simply enjoying a book. While we hesitate to deem this approach creative, we must acknowledge that it is rarely observed in classrooms.

For another example, we present the idea of having "book talks." Ask a few students each day to do book talks. This is where they choose a book and tell the class about it. Some of the requirements might be that they state the title, show the illustration on the cover, and point out some of their favorite illustrations throughout the book. You can then observe their ability to identify the book title, locate the front cover, and open the book correctly and turn the pages. Not only does this make a great artful assessment, but it serves as a daily model of concepts about print for your class. We also like this informal assessment because it includes an affective component – students are required to think about their book preferences and what they like about these books. We encourage you to think about more ways that concepts about print can be assessed in authentic, aesthetic, and creative ways.

Initial Reading and Decoding

In the initial reading and decoding stage, students begin to understand that oral and written language are connected. That is, the sounds and words they hear can be represented as letters and words in print. At this point, students begin to crack the alphabetic code. They start to connect sounds to letters and connect words they hear to words on a page. In this stage, students begin to read simple texts containing regularly spelled words and basic sight words. It is the magical stage where you can see students begin to read.

Assessments in this stage typically assess phonemic awareness, phonics, sight words, and accuracy in reading. Phonemic awareness is often assessed one-on-one in order to determine how well students can orally manipulate sounds by assessing their ability to isolate, blend, segment, and delete sounds in words. The assessments will also test students' ability to rhyme words. A teacher will sit with a student and direct them through an assessment similar to the one shown in Figure 8.2.

In this stage, you will also assess your students' alphabetic and phonics knowledge. When assessing alphabetic knowledge, it is as simple as asking your student to name the letters of the alphabet on a page and marking

	Prompt	Correct? ✔ / X
Isolate	What sound do you hear at the beginning of *bag*?	
	What sound do you hear at the end of *bag*?	
	What sound do you hear in the beginning of *bag*?	
	Isolate Total Correct	/3
Blend	I am going to slowly say some sounds. Put them together and tell me what word you hear.	
	/c/ /a/ /t/	
	/b/ /i/ /g/	
	/t/ /u/ /b/	
	Blend Total Correct	/3
Segment	I will say a word and you break it into the sounds you hear.	
	Dog	
	Sit	
	Name	
	Segment Total Correct	/3
Delete	Say the word *get* without the /g/ sound.	
	Say the word *run* without the /u/ sound.	
	Say the word *map* without the /p/ sound.	
	Delete Total Correct	/3
Rhyme	Does the word *play* rhyme with *may*?	
	Does the word *happy* rhyme with *time*?	
	What word rhymes with *dad*? (Take any correct answer.)	
	Rhyme Total Correct	/3
	Total Correct	**/15**

Figure 8.2 Sample phonemic awareness assessment.

whether they know the letter or not. The assessment is often done with both lowercase and uppercase letters. An example of the uppercase letter identification assessment is in Figure 8.3.

Now that you have assessed the child's ability to identify letters, it is time to assess their ability to identify the sounds of each letter. Keep in mind that some letters have multiple sounds. Thus, the assessment page may look the same as Figure 8.3, but the teacher record form will point out

Assessment directions: Sit with your student and ask them to identify the letters on the page. Use your own copy of the assessment to mark whether the student accurately identified the letter.

Q	W	E	R	T
Y	U	I	O	P
A	S	D	F	G
H	J	K	L	Z
X	C	V	B	N
M	**Total Correct: ___/26**			

Figure 8.3 Uppercase letter identification assessment.

Q	W	E (2 pts)	R	T
Y (2 pts)	U (2 pts)	I (2 pts)	O (2 pts)	P
A (2 pts)	S	D	F	G
H	J	K	L	Z
X	C	V	B	N
M	**Total Correct: ___/32**			

Figure 8.4 Letter sound identification.

that some letters should be double-scored if the student is able to produce both sounds (Figure 8.4).

Unfortunately, Figure 8.3, "Uppercase letter identification assessment," is not very aesthetic. It is, again, very much a teacher/student assessment setup. You can imagine sitting at the teacher's desk saying the letters as you see them. As a student, you are not sure what you are doing there, and you may not even care. To that, we ask, why do letter identification assessments have to be on paper? After all, students are quite used to using color magnetic letters or finger painting to learn their letters – why do we not assess them that way? Maybe because the term "assessment" drains authenticity, aesthetics, and creativity out of teachers' brains. Of course, that is just a theory.

You know from the phonics chapter that phonics is a monster of a reading component. More assessments are needed to determine your students' advanced phonics skills, such as knowledge of blends, digraphs, schwas, and diphthongs, as well as their ability to decode common phonetic spelling patterns, such as consonant-vowel-consonant (CVC), CV, VC, CCVC, CVCC, CVCe, or CVVC. A brief example assessing a few of these is shown in Figure 8.5.

Phonics assessments can get long and detailed to assess the many required skills that serve as a foundation for reading. In addition to the decoding skills, you will also want to assess a student's sight word knowledge. According to Vaughn and Linan-Thompson (2004), there are 30 irregular and common sight words that beginning readers should master,

Word	Skill(s) Assessed	Correct? ✔ / X
Mud	CVC: Student reads word with short vowel sound.	
Fud	CVC: Student reads nonsense word with short vowel sound.	
So	CV: Student reads word with long vowel sound.	
Vo	CV: Student reads nonsense word with long vowel sound.	
At	VC: Student reads word with short vowel sound.	
Af	VC: Student reads nonsense word with short vowel sound.	
Kite	CVCe: Student reads word with long vowel.	
Dite	CVCe: Student reads nonsense word with long vowel.	
Star	CCVC: Student reads word with short vowel. Blend: Student blends /st/.	
Stap	CCVC: Student reads nonsense word with short vowel sound. Blend: Student blends /st/.	
Math	CVCC: Student reads word with short vowel. Digraph: Student reads digraph /th/ correctly.	
Guth	CVCC: Student reads nonsense word with short vowel. Digraph: Student reads digraph /th/ correctly.	
Beat	CVVC: Student reads word with long vowel. Digraph: Student reads /ea/ as one sound.	
Rean	CVVC: Student reads nonsense word with long vowel. Digraph: Student reads /ea/ as one sound.	

Figure 8.5 Common spelling pattern assessment.

which therefore should also be assessed. Like the other assessments, print two copies and mark which words a student reads correctly.

Of course, these words are only recommended by some people who do not know your students or context, and you as a teacher can decide which sight words appear most frequently in texts, or which words students tend to find most challenging to recall. Or, you might decide to revise it based on what you are teaching. For example, if you are teaching a unit on communities (and you think it is weird that *whose* is on the list), your list may look more like the one in Figure 8.7. As a bonus, the unusual addition of the word *whose* is no longer included. In what world is *whose* a frequently encountered sight word in primer stories? You may also notice that these words are not necessarily all irregularly spelled. It is your assessment, so assess what you want.

For more advanced students, you may want to assess their recognition of Greek and Latin roots. Being able to recognize commonly used Greek and Latin roots can be quite helpful when decoding new words, especially

the	you	said	his	people
to	they	were	do	know
was	would	are	some	your
of	there	because	as	mother
is	one	what	could	who
two	too	should	put	whose

Figure 8.6 Irregularly spelled sight words for beginning readers.

the	you	said	classroom	town
to	they	were	home	street
was	would	are	live	neighbor
of	there	because	park	city
is	one	what	job	school
two	too	should	family	help

Figure 8.7 Sight word and community unit words assessment.

Mod	Bio	Phon
Geo	Multi	Poly
Hyper	Mal	Non

Figure 8.8 Greek and Latin root word recognition assessment.

because so many words contain roots, which can later be used in vocabulary instruction. A brief example can be found in Figure 8.8.

Essentially, there are many useful assessments to be used in the initial decoding stage, but not of all of them will give you the information you really need. Therefore, you are free to modify them to suit the needs of your students as well as to inform your instruction. This was not a comprehensive list of assessments or examples to be used during the initial reading and decoding stage, but we hope it gives you some ideas on how assessments can be used with students who are beginning to read as well as ideas on how they can be modified. In the next section, we explore the next stage according to Chall.

Confirmation and Fluency Stage

In this stage, students begin to apply their learning in previous stages and develop into more fluent readers. That is, students can integrate their recognition of sight words with their more automatic decoding skills to read more seamlessly through text. As students become more fluent, it is often easier for them to understand the texts. Thus, at this stage of regarding assessment, we want to examine their ability to read fluently and with comprehension. To properly assess fluency, we assess each of its components – accuracy, automaticity, and prosody.

Accuracy is simply assessed by computing a percentage of words read correctly. As students read, we mark any word recognition errors. After the reading, we divide the number of words read correctly by the number of words that were read, which produces a percentage. If we are attempting to determine a student's independent reading level, ideally students should be able to read a high percentage of words accurately. Consider the following example (Figure 8.9). Ms. McClure asks Brooklynn, a first grader, to

> Kristen loves to read. She sits in her room all day and reads her books. One day, her dad ~~hid~~ all her books. She ~~could~~ not find them. It was a sad day for Kristen. Her dad ~~felt~~ bad and gave her the books back. She began to read again.

Figure 8.9 Running record for word recognition accuracy.

read the following (lame) story out loud. The teacher listens and marks any words that Brooklynn says incorrectly.

The teacher marked three errors out of 49 words. Thus, the student read 46 words correctly. To compute the percentage, we divide 46 by 49, which equals about 94 percent accuracy. That may sound good to you, or not so good to you. How does it sound to us? It simply sounds like the student read with 94 percent accuracy. What we do with that information to plan instruction is what matters.

Some students can read with less accuracy and still understand the text completely. Conversely, some students can read with 100 percent accuracy and not understand very well. Here is where we have a discrepancy between the science and art, which further demonstrates the claim that teaching and even assessing reading goes beyond science. The International Literacy Association (ILA, 2018) admits that "precisely defined standards for reading accuracy have not been scientifically established." However, the brief goes on to recommend at least 95 percent accuracy for most students, and even higher for younger students (at least 97 or 98 percent). These guidelines have been around for most of our careers in reading education and can be misconstrued as an exact science. This is where artful assessment and interpretation of the results is necessary.

According to the recommendation by ILA, Brooklynn's word recognition accuracy would prevent her from being considered independent on that level of text by one percent. If it were the end of the year, should we hold her back? Send her to summer school? Maybe. Maybe not. This is only one component of reading fluency. We also need to measure the words read correctly per minute (WCPM), or her reading automaticity. While the teacher was listening to her reading accuracy, Ms. McClure had also timed her reading. To determine WCPM, we use the following formula:

(Words Read Correctly x 60) / Number of Seconds Read = WCPM

Brooklyn read the story in 35 seconds and she read 46 words correctly. Therefore, the equation would look like this:

$$(46 \times 60) / 35 = 78.86$$

The number of words read correctly was 46, and we multiply it by 60, which equaled 2,760. After dividing by the total number of seconds it took Brooklynn to read the entire text (35), we see that she read the text at about 79 words per minute after rounding. Great, what does that mean? Informally speaking, she read at a pretty good pace. More formally, and perhaps scientifically, we consult the oral reading fluency norms (Hasbrouck & Tindal, 2017). Brooklynn read this passage in the spring of her first grade year. According to the oral reading fluency norms chart (which you can search for on the Web), the average expectation for a first grader in the spring is 60 WCPM. Therefore, Brooklynn's reading automaticity is above the norm, and is approaching the 75th percentile.

So far, we know that Brooklynn reads with 94 percent accuracy and at 79 words correct per minute on this particular (lame) text. The final measure of fluency is prosody, which is the reading research "nerd word" for reading expression. While Ms. McClure was marking errors and timing Brooklynn's reading, she was also listening to her expressive reading. Most commonly, reading prosody is assessed using a rubric, such as the one below (Table 7.1). While reading, Ms. McClure noticed that Brooklynn read in phrases, used expression at times, and attended to punctuation appropriately, which is best described as a three on the fluency rubric.

Now, we know that Brooklynn reads with decent accuracy, proficient prosody, and excellent automaticity. While she might be below the "expectation" in accuracy, she makes up for it in other areas. Of course, the assessment process is not done. We consider her fluency, but we also need to measure her reading comprehension to get the full picture of her reading proficiency. While this obviously can be and should be measured in this stage, we will discuss the comprehension assessment aspect after introducing Chall's next stage.

Table 7.1 NAEP ORF Rubric

Fluent	Level 4	Reads primarily in larger, meaningful phrase groups. Although some regressions, repetitions, and deviations from text may be present, these do not appear to detract from the overall structure of the story. Preservation of the author's syntax is consistent. Some or most of the story is read with expressive interpretation.
	Level 3	Reads primarily in three- or four-word phrase groups. Some small groupings may be present. However, the majority of phrasing seems appropriate and preserves the syntax of the author. Little or no expressive interpretation is present.
Nonfluent	Level 2	Reads primarily in two-word phrases with some three- or four-word groupings. Some word-by-word reading may be present. Word groupings may seem awkward and unrelated to larger context of sentence or passage.
	Level 1	Reads primarily word by word. Occasional two-word or three-word phrases may occur – but these are infrequent and/or they do not preserve meaningful syntax.

Source: US Department of Education, Institute of Education Sciences, National Center for Education Statistics, National Assessment of Educational Progress (NAEP), 2002 Oral Reading Study

Reading for Learning the New

While this stage sounds relatively formal, a rearranging of words describes the stage fairly accurately: "Reading to Learn." No, this stage is not limited to nonfiction learning only. As students read any genre, they build background knowledge, gain experiences, improve vocabulary, learn facts, become familiar with text structure, and gain experience to decipher more challenging texts. In this stage, a primary focus is for students to refine their foundational skills and focus on reading comprehension – the goal of reading.

We now return to Brooklynn. Traditional reading comprehension assessments follow the oral or silent reading of a text. Commonly, those assessments are in the form of a retell, answering questions, or both. Here is what an example might look like for the story about the stolen books.

There are five questions, three of which are explicit, meaning that they ask questions about the text directly. Two of the questions (*Why was Kristen sad? Why did her dad feel bad?*) are implicit questions. These two questions ask the student to infer or process the text in order to give an accurate response. These questions are sometimes paired with a retell, and we ask the student to tell us the events they remember in order. With these two measures, we get a decent idea of whether they understood and can recall what they read.

Now we revisit our example. Brooklynn answered all the explicit questions, and she was able to tell each event in order when retelling the story. However, she missed both implicit questions. Thus, we determine she can recall what she reads but may have trouble inferring. To summarize, she read a first grade level text with reasonable fluency and comprehension

---

Kristen loves to read. She sits in her room all day and reads her books. One day, her dad hid all her books. She could not find them. It was a sad day for Kristen. Her dad felt bad and gave her the books back. She began to read again.

Questions: Answer the questions about the story.	Retell: Start at the beginning and tell me what happened in this story.
☐ What does Kristen love to do?	☐ Kristen was reading in her room.
☐ What did her dad do?	☐ Her dad hid the books.
☐ Why was Kristen sad?	☐ Kristen could not find the books.
☐ Why did her dad feel bad?	☐ Her dad gave the books back.
☐ What did Kristen do when she got her books back?	☐ She began to read again.
___ Total correct	___ Total correct

Figure 8.10 Measuring reading comprehension.

but missed the inferring questions. Does she pass? We believe so, despite her word recognition accuracy that was below the somewhat arbitrary 95 percent expectation. We have also determined that she needs additional implicit reading comprehension instruction.

Of course, there are many other boring and scientific ways to assess reading comprehension, including standardized tests, which are beyond the scope of this book, and therefore we will skip all of that and address some examples of ways that you can artfully assess your students in reading comprehension. Most of these involve direct observation of authentic and creative ways to demonstrate their understandings of texts.

Book Talks

We mentioned earlier in the chapter how book talks could be used to assess concepts about print, but they can certainly be used to assess reading comprehension as well. We select a few students each day to talk about a book they read or are reading. In this case, however, we want them to choose a book they read during independent reading or at home the night before. That is because we want to assess their current reading comprehension, not their comprehension of a book they read 40 times three years prior in kindergarten. For the comprehension-based book talks, we might require students to state the title, the main idea, some key details, and their overall impression of the book. There are plenty of requirements that you might add, such as how the book made them feel, how they might change the book, how the book changed their thinking, what they liked or disliked about the book, and the list goes on. You might even give them the choice of what they would like to share in addition to some basic information.

Reading and Talking with Your Students

Finally, recall the anecdote at the beginning of this chapter about Mr. Parsons and Archer. Reading and talking with your students about their reading is a powerful way to monitor their progress. During independent reading is a perfect time to quickly conference with your students. Indeed, there are spelling tests to grade, but this time is ripe for assessing reading comprehension, among other aspects of reading. Indeed, there are children who willingly isolate themselves for hours with a good book. However, there are many more who only engage when they hear, "Hey, let's read a book." To them, it is a social practice. There is an increase in computer-based reading assessments and teachers are pressed for time; we fear that the combination may decrease the amount of time teachers spend listening to their students read and engage in conversations. We believe that these conversations are critical for assessing and teaching reading. You can gain so much by listening to them read and talking about what they understand about texts.

Creative Demonstration of Comprehension

Reenactments. Student can create reenactments of their readings. This can be of an entire book, or perhaps a chapter. They can direct a group of students or they can reenact it themselves. This can be a great way to assess students' understandings of text, and it is usually entertaining.

Student-Produced Movies. As described in beginning of this book, when a student finishes a book they love, they can make it into a movie. Simple as that. They create script treatments, storyboards, and scripts and conduct the filming and editing process. The assessment is actually a movie premiere, and it is far more entertaining than grading multiple-choice exams. For more on making movies, see Young and Rasinski (2013). We uploaded their movies to the Internet, and kids who are now grown still visit and watch their movies. That's right. Our students stare at their old comprehension assessments nostalgically – something you have probably never done nor care to.

Writing Parodies. We believe that being able to write good parodies of texts is an indicator of deep understanding. To successfully write a parody, the student must first understand the author's purpose in the original text. Then, to make it hilarious, the student must carefully shift that purpose by making subtle changes throughout the text. It really is a great way to deeply analyze texts (for more on that, see Young & Rasinski, 2011). You can then read the prosody and determine whether is follows the original texts. We have read some good ones in the past, some of which we copied and kept forever. When is the last time you did that with a student's reading comprehension assessment?

Comic Strips. After reading a text, students transpose the text into a comic strip. This allows them to determine which key events should be included and essentially create a visual representation of the sequence of events. As a bonus, the students also get to spend time drawing and coloring – two things we believe there should be more of in elementary school. We promise that the comic strip will look better on their parent's fridge than a multiple-choice test about bad traffic.

Write the Author. Now, here is a great way to promote authenticity in reading assessment. We have our students prepare a letter for the author describing what the student liked about the text. After you review the letter and assess whether they understood the story, you can help them send it via email or snail mail. We used to do this all the time, and the students often got responses. Mo Willems once sent a thank-you card with a hand drawing of the pigeon. How cool is that? I promise that if you write Pearson about their state standardized test passages, they will not send you a drawing.

Anything. Teachers, you are free to come up with hundreds more of these. We hope that some of these examples opened your eyes to the possibility of assessing your students' reading comprehension in authentic, creative, and aesthetic ways.

Conclusion

In this chapter, we presented some scientific ways to assess different aspects of reading. We also presented ways to tweak those assessments to be more artful. Finally, we showed you how to completely unglue yourself from traditional assessments and embrace more authentic, aesthetic, and creative ways to measure reading comprehension. Let's bring you back to Earth. There is a need for all of these. Scientific approaches are useful in many ways and so are the more artful approaches. Keep this in mind when selecting and using assessments. We believe that effective reading assessments benefit both the teacher and the student. If you keep that in mind, you are going to be just fine. Assess your children well.

References

Chall, J. (1996). *Stages of reading development* (2nd ed.). Fort Worth, TX: Harcourt-Brace.

Hasbrouck, J., & Tindal, G. (2017). *An update to compiled ORF norms (technical report no. 1702)*. Eugene, OR: Behavioral Research and Teaching, University of Oregon.

International Literacy Association. (2018). *Reading fluently does not mean reading fast [literacy leadership brief]*. Newark, DE: Author.

Vaughn, S., & Linan-Thompson, S. (2004). *Research-based methods of reading instruction*. Alexandria, VA: Association for Supervision and Curriculum Development.

Young, C., & Rasinski, T. (2011). Enhancing authors' voice through scripting. *Reading Teacher, 65*(1), 24–28.

Young, C., & Rasinski, T. (2013). Student produced movies as a medium for literacy development. *Reading Teacher, 66*(8), 670–675.

Artful Approaches to Home and Family Reading

Addelaide was excited. After several weeks of performing with two other classmates in her second grade classroom's weekly Readers' Theater Festival, she decided that this week, she would perform solo. Since it was nearing Halloween, Addy chose a "spooky" poem to perform for her classmates and other classroom visitors. Of course, Mrs. Robinson gave the class time during the school days during the week to rehearse their texts, but she also reminded the students that most of the rehearsal should be done at home where students could practice with and perform for family members.

Addy's parents were on top of it. They had woven her home rehearsal into the everyday fabric of family life. As soon as she came home from school, Addy would perform for her older brother. As Dad was preparing dinner, Addy would perform for him. And, when Mom came home from work, one of the first things she wanted to do was listen to Addy's performance after saying hello to the family. With each performance, family members praised Addy's performance and also gave feedback to her reading: "Be sure to stand straight and tall," "Use a loud voice," "Slow down here," "Emphasize this word," "Make a dramatic pause right here." All told, from Monday to Thursday, Addelaide read her poem to family members a total of 14 times! She also thinks she read it another ten times in school. Talk about repeated readings!

On Friday's Readers' Theater Festival, Addy's parents were there and beamed with pride as their daughter was one of the classroom stars with her performance. Listening to Addy perform with expression, confidence, and joy, one could hardly believe that she had struggled with reading in first grade.

Making It Artful

We have written this book under the premise that to be truly effective developing proficient and lifelong readers, reading instruction needs to be science based and artful. We have defined "scientific reading instruction" as instruction that falls into the categories identified by the National Reading Panel (2000) (phonemic awareness, phonics or word recognition, vocabulary or word meaning, fluency, and comprehension) and that is validated by evidence-based research.

When involving families in children's reading development, teachers have wonderful opportunities to be artful as well as scientific. In this chapter, we offer examples of just how this might be done.

Maximizing Reading

Interestingly, the National Reading Panel (2000) did not include voluntary reading as one of its scientifically validated tenets of effective literacy instruction. Although there is a plethora of correlational research that clearly demonstrates that the more students read, the higher are their levels of reading proficiency, the National Reading Panel relied primarily on causal research in making its determination of key scientific components of effective reading instruction. In a review of recent research on reading volume, Allington and McGill-Franzen (2021) make a compelling case that the amount of reading one does is essential for reading growth and success. Thus, we include maximizing reading volume as a scientific tenet for effective instruction in school and home. Moreover, not only is maximizing voluntary reading science based, the very nature of voluntary reading is an artful approach to improving students' literacy achievement. Voluntary reading meets the artful criteria of being authentic – it is something that adult proficient readers do regularly and extensively for a variety of authentic purposes: to entertain, to learn, to solve problems, to communicate, and so on.

The issue, then, is not that maximizing voluntary reading at home is important, but how can teachers and schools work to increase the amount of reading students do at home (and school)? The research indicates that students, on average, do not read much at home. In a study of upper elementary grade students who were asked to keep track of their at-home reading, Anderson, Wilson, and Fielding (1988) reported that, on average, students read approximately ten minutes per night at home. Clearly, that is not very much reading. Reading at a rate of 120 words per minute, that amounts to slightly over 1,000 words per day. This study was done in 1988; more recent reports indicate that the voluntary reading of books has dramatically declined over the past half century (National Endowment for the Arts, 2004, 2007).

One approach to increasing voluntary reading was inspired by a television game show (*Who Wants to Be a Millionaire?*) and a worldwide challenge (Ice Bucket Challenge) (O'Masta & Wolf, 1991; Rasinski & Padak, 2011; Shanahan, Wojciechowski, & Rubik, 1998). To implement "Who Wants to Be a (Reading) Millionaire?," teachers in a school simply determined the total number of minutes read at home if every student (in kindergarten through fifth grade) read for at least 20 minutes at home every day during the school year (180 days). The 20-minute goal per night for reading was based on the notion of doubling the amount of reading actually done, on average, at home. The assumption is that doubling the amount of reading should lead to increases in reading achievement. So, in a school of 300 students, if all students read (or, for kindergarteners and early first grade students, were read to) 20 minutes per evening for 180 school days, the total amount of reading over the course of the school year would come to slightly over a million minutes. Of course, the goal in terms of minutes read would have to be adjusted depending on the number of students and the duration of the project (it could be done over the summer months).

Parents would be asked to model reading at home for their children, encourage their children to read, and keep weekly records of their children's reading that would be sent to the school. Weekly tallies of individual classrooms and grade levels could lead to friendly competitions between grades or classrooms. At the end of the school year, if the goal was achieved, a victory celebration would be provided for the school community and various individual or group awards could be made.

The goal of a project such as this is simply to encourage the school community to engage in achieving a common goal. As in any endeavor that is done as a team effort, when students feel like a part of a team (school, grade level, classroom), they are more likely to engage in the activity. And if they read more, reading achievement is certain to improve.

In addition to encouraging children to read independently, the simple act of parents reading to their children regularly holds immense potential for improving reading outcomes. In a classic study of children who started school already knowing how to read, Dolores Durkin (1966) reported that one of the most common features of early readers was parents who read to their children regularly! But even once children have entered school and are beginning to read, reading to children should remain a priority for home as well as school. When parents read to children, they can read texts that are above the children's own ability to read on their own. This will expose children to more sophisticated words and more complex texts, both of which are certain to improve language comprehension. Moreover, when parents read to their children, they are modeling their own value of reading, and also providing their children with a model of fluent oral reading. And, perhaps the best part of parents reading to their children is just the close bonding that occurs when parent and child sit side by side and share a good story. Parents reading aloud to children should be at the top of any list of recommendations for parents to support their children's reading.

Of course, there are many other ways to foster reading at home. The key, however, is to be proactive and creative and to develop something that students (and families) find authentic, effective, and engaging. That is the challenge of being an instructional artist and scientist.

Communication Is Key

Beyond encouraging parents to read to their children and to maximize their children's own reading, communicating with parents is probably the most important way for teachers to support children's literacy development at home. It is often the case when parents are not kept informed about what is happening in the school and how they can support what is happening in the school and classroom that difficulties arise. Keeping parents and families informed not only about what their children are learning in school, but also how they can support their children at home, will pay dividends in the long run. A classic study of reading achievement worldwide found that the number one variable associated with reading achievement in the world was parental involvement (Postlethwaite & Ross, 1992). Teachers who work to create partnerships with the families of their students in reading were more likely to have students who were more proficient in reading.

Communication can take a variety of forms. A monthly one- or two-page newsletter can inform parents of what students have been doing in the classroom in literacy instruction and provide suggestions for how parents can support their children in these efforts. Such a newsletter can provide suggestions for parents that go beyond the classroom instruction to how they can support their children independently in the key areas of reading during the school year and even into the vacation months. Moreover, newsletters can also be a great way to celebrate students' literacy accomplishments through the publication of their writings to descriptions of their various projects. Of course, as technology has advanced, the ability to communicate to parents can take a variety of novel forms. Electronic newsletters, email blasts, classroom websites, and such allow teachers much greater flexibility in communicating with parents – not just the written word, but also opportunities to share information and accomplishments orally with parents and other family members. In the sections below, we offer some ideas on what can be communicated to parents in the critical literacy competencies.

Phonemic Awareness

Developing phonemic awareness, the awareness and ability to manipulate discrete sounds of language, along with letter knowledge, is fundamental to phonics and reading in general. In much the same way that teachers can promote phonemics in the classroom, teachers can also help parents and family members promote phonemic awareness at home.

Most parents of young children are not aware of the nature of phonemic awareness and its importance in reading development. Thus, key to developing phonemic awareness at home is education for parents of children in prekindergarten through early first grade. A simple one-hour workshop in school, and also recorded for access at home through the

Internet, can help in understanding the nature of phonemic awareness, its importance in phonics and general reading development, and ways in which it can be nurtured at home.

Simple activities that model the use of nursery rhymes, poems, songs, tongue twisters, and turtle talk with young children are demonstrated to parents in such a workshop. After a demonstration, parents themselves can be asked to do the same with their children. Similarly, sound manipulation activities ("What do you get when you take the /t/ off of *tip*?" "If I add /s/ to *cat*, what word do I get?") can also be described and modeled for parents and other family members such as grandparents and siblings if they are so inclined. The beauty of such activities is that they can be done in an informal and gamelike fashion in the midst of normal family life – while making or eating dinner, during bath time, at bedtime, when calling Grandma on the phone, and so on. Regular communication to parents of new ideas for phonemic awareness at home is sure to pay dividends when students move into formal phonics instruction.

Phonics and Word Study

Words are important, and enlisting parents' help in developing their children's word recognition skills is crucial for their literacy development. One of the easiest ways and most authentic ways to involve families in word study is through games. Recall that many families, on their own, play games that involve words – Scrabble, Boggle, Wheel of Fortune, and the like. Sharing with parents word study games that are appropriate for students and that have a focus on word structure (phonics and spelling) and meaning (vocabulary) can make word study fun and engaging for all involved and can lead to growth in word mastery.

WORDO! is a bingo-like game where instead of having a number in each of the blocks of a player's card, there are words that are in the process of being taught. These could be words involved in phonics and spelling instruction, words for expanding vocabularies, or words related to a particular content area of instruction. One member of the family acts as the host while other family members have a blank card (either a three-by-three, four-by-four, or five-by-five matrix). The host provides players with a list of words for the game, and players write one word in each square in the matrix wherever they wish. Then, the host randomly chooses words from the original list and either pronounces the word or gives a meaningful clue to the word. If the player has the word on their card, they cover it with a chip or marker. As with bingo, the first player who gets a vertical, horizontal, or diagonal line of chips on their card calls out the name of the game – in this case, "WORDO!" – and is declared the winner. Players clear their cards and a new game can commence. WORDO! provides a great opportunity to practice recognizing words that may be under instruction in school. It also allows for practice in deepening students' understanding of words.

Fluency

Paired reading is a fluency development activity in which a student orally reads a text simultaneously with a more fluent partner. The more fluent partner provides a scaffold for the student by using their oral reading as a model and support for the student's reading. Developed by Keith Topping (1987, 1989, 1995) originally as simple and time efficient parent involvement activity, Topping's research found that ten minutes per day of paired reading could accelerate a student's progress in reading by a factor of three to five. By this, we mean that a student who previously was making, for example, half a month's progress in reading for a month's worth of instruction would now make between one and a half month's progress to two and a half month's progress when doing paired reading. Moreover, the progress was not just in terms of fluency, but overall proficiency in reading.

The rules for doing paired reading are quite simple. The student chooses the book or text to read (owner and choice are always important). The student and partner sit side by side so that the student can hear their partner's voice. As they read together, the student uses a finger to point to the text as it is read. When the student wants to "solo" read for a while, they give a predetermined signal to the partner (such as a tap on the wrist). The partner stops reading orally but follows along silently. This continues until the student either signals for the partner to jump back in orally or to go back to oral reading if the student begins to experience some difficulty. At the end of the reading, student and partner discuss what they have read together and also chat about the actual reading and areas of difficulty.

The simplicity and authenticity of paired reading make it easy to teach parents. An hour of instruction in person or through a video is usually all that is needed. Indeed, several YouTube videos are available that provide excellent demonstrations of paired reading. In addition to its instructional efficacy, paired reading provides a great opportunity for parents (or other family members) to connect with their children.

In our chapter on fluency, we described the notion of regular classroom performances of poetry, songs, and scripts as authentic opportunities to make use of repeated and assisted reading in the classroom. This approach can easily extend to families and home involvement. If students will be performing a selected text at the end of each week, rehearsal (repeated readings) can take place at home as well as in the classroom. Parents and other family members can be asked to listen to their children's rehearsals and provide formative feedback at home on a nightly basis for as little as ten minutes. If the selected texts are a bit challenging for students, the rehearsal can go beyond listening to the students' reading to modeling the reading for the student and engaging in paired reading with the student. The activity is authentic in that there is a real purpose to the activity – to perform for an audience at the end of the week. Moreover, the ultimate form of parental and home involvement can occur when parents them-selves are invited to come to their student's actual performance.

Comprehension

Comprehension is often fostered through conversations when we chat with one another about what we have read. If you've ever belonged to a book club, you likely experienced a deeper understanding of the books you read as a group by engaging in conversations with others. You and the other members of the group asked and responded to interesting questions and offered insights that deepened your comprehension. Certainly, parents can be encouraged to engage in conversations with their children about what they are reading. The problem is that many parents are not aware of how they can engage their children in productive discussion. This is where teachers can take the lead in communicating with parents. Perhaps a simple set of possible questions are just the thing to get parent-child reading discussions off to a productive start. Here's a list of questions we

How are _____ and _____ alike?
How are you like or unlike the character in this story?
How is this story like another story we have read?
What is the main idea of _____?
What do you think would happen if _____?
What are the strengths and weakness of _____?
In what way is _____ related to _____?
How does _____ affect _____?
Compare _____ and _____ with regard to _____.
What do you think causes _____?
How does _____ tie in with what we have learned or read before?
Which one is the best _____ and why?
What are some possible solutions for the problem of _____?
Do you agree or disagree with this statement: _____. Why?
What do you still not understand about _____?

Figure 9.1 Questions to promote discussion and deepen comprehension.

have shared with parents in the past that have been quite helpful in getting children to think more deeply and creatively about the texts they read (or texts that are read to them by parents).

Reading (and Writing)

This book is primarily about the teaching of reading in ways that are artful as well as scientific. However, it is clear that writing is part of the reading process, and years of scientific research have demonstrated that reading and writing are linked. When a person writes, they are also reading, and that written text is likely to be read by another person. How can parents engage with their children in writing?

Journaling has long been advocated as an excellent way for students to engage in personal and reflective writing. Many teachers have students maintain a journal throughout the school year and write entries in their journal at the end of each day.

Dialogue journaling is a different sort of journal. A dialogue journal is kept between two participants such as parent and child. Essentially, it is a way for a parent and child to communicate with one another in a different mode – a journal or notebook.

Here's how it works. The parent begins the dialogue journal by writing a note to their child in a notebook. It usually starts out very informally but over time can lead to some quite personal and important topics. Once the parent completes their note, they give it to their daughter or son, often by simply laying it on the child's bed. The child then reads the note from the parent and responds to the parent's note and adds their own message – often a question, idea, or suggestion. The child returns the journal notebook to the parent (setting it on the bed or other place where the parent will find it) and the cycle begins again. In essence, a dialogue journal is a conversation between child and parent.

But many good things can happen with dialogue journaling. First and foremost, dialogue journaling is authentic and purposeful writing and reading for both parent and child. Both child and parent have opportunities to express themselves in much deeper ways than are usually available through spoken conversations. There is something profound (and permanent) about writing something. The dialogue journal also acts as a model of journal or letter writing for the child. The child, in reading the parent's entries, will no doubt examine how the parent structures their entries and will try to emulate the parent's writing. Finally, and perhaps most importantly, the dialogue journal becomes a wonderful tool for parent and child to further deepen their relationship with one another. As the years pass by, that dialogue journal will be a treasured keepsake and a record of a child's relationship with a parent. It doesn't get much better than that.

Of course, teachers can engage in dialogue journaling with their students as well. But inviting parents to do the same with their own children is an opportunity that should not be missed. Most parents do not know about this form of writing, so it is up to the artful teacher to present it to parents.

Making Partnerships

Parents usually have plenty on their plates. Certainly, it is fully reasonable to ask and expect parents to be involved in their children's learning and literacy development. There is much that parents can do. At the same time, we need to be mindful of those things that are on parents' plates as well. Our job is not to "tell" parents what to do, but to invite them into a partnership with us in creating the best possible outcomes for their children. And we do this by communicating regularly with parents about ways in which they can engage with their children on nurturing literacy and a love of reading in their children.

References

Allington, R. L., & McGill-Franzen, A. M. (2021). Reading volume and reading achievement: A review of recent research. *Read Res Q*, 56(S1), S231–S238. https://doi.org/10.1002/rrq.404

Anderson, R. C., Wilson, P. T., & Fielding, L. G. (1988). Growth in reading and how children spend their time outside of school. *Reading Research Quarterly, 23*, 285–303.

Durkin, D. (1966). *Children who read early: Two longitudinal studies*. New York: Teachers College Press.

National Endowment for the Arts. (2004). *Reading at risk: A survey of literary reading in America (Research Division Report No. 46)*. Washington, DC: Author.

National Endowment for the Arts. (2007). *To read or not to read: A question of national consequence (Research Division Report No. 47)*. Washington, DC: Author.

National Reading Panel. (2000). *Teaching children to read: An evidence-based assessment of the scientific research literature on reading and its implications for reading instruction. National institute of health pub. No. 00–4769*. Washington, DC: National Institute of Child Health and Human Development.

O'Masta, G. A., & Wolf, J. A. (1991). Encouraging independent reading through the reading millionaires project. *The Reading Teacher, 44*(9), 656–662.

Postlethwaite, T. N., & Ross, K. N. (1992). *Effective schools in reading: Implications for policy planner*. The Hague: International Association for the Evaluation of Educational Achievement.

Rasinski, T. V., & Padak, N. (2011). Who wants to be a (reading) millionaire? *The Reading Teacher, 64*, 553–555. https://doi.org/10.1598/RT.64.7.14

Shanahan, S., Wojciechowski, J., & Rubik, G. (1998). A celebration of reading: How our school read for one million minutes. *The Reading Teacher, 52*, 93–96.

Topping, K. (1987). Paired reading: A powerful technique for parent use. *The Reading Teacher, 40*, 604–614.

Topping, K. (1989). Peer tutoring and paired reading. Combining two powerful techniques. *The Reading Teacher, 42*, 488–494.

Topping, K. (1995). *Paired reading, spelling, and writing*. New York: Cassell.

Using Reading Models, Theories, and Research to Develop Effective and Artful Reading Instruction and Interventions

 ## Introduction

The purpose of this final chapter is to empower teachers to use their knowledge of theories, research, and experience to develop their own effective and artful approaches to reading instruction. We will reflect on the previous chapters and examine a couple prominent theories and models in reading to demonstrate how teachers can create activities and interventions to best meet the needs of their students. We hope this chapter will empower you as teachers to not only use what has been validated by the science of reading, but to create new and engaging ways that are worthy of future research and eventual inclusion into the many scientifically supported options for reading teachers.

 ## Models and Theories of Reading

We begin by describing a few models and theories of reading that we can consider while developing artful and effective approaches to teaching reading. The Simple View of Reading (Gough & Tunmer, 1986) claims that

DOI: 10.4324/9781003218609-10

reading is a combination of knowing how to decode and understanding language. Many of the advocates of the scientific view of reading and reading instruction embrace this view. It is often presented as a formula:

Decoding + language comprehension = reading comprehension

Indeed, this is a simple view, and intuitively it makes sense. Students combine their ability to recognize words in print with their knowledge of the word in speech, and they are able to accurately pronounce the word and also determine its meaning. Of course, reading word by word may not support reading comprehension sufficiently, so we can expand the Simple View to the following formula:

The ability to decode words with accuracy and with automaticity + the ability to understand oral language = reading comprehension

It makes a lot of sense and gives teachers the big picture when approaching reading instruction. That is, we make sure we are developing students' oral language skills along with their ability to decode print fluently. The automaticity theory fits nicely here, knowing that as readers become more automatic in word recognition, they can focus their energy on understanding the text (LaBerge & Samuels, 1974).

However, there are components of these major processes in the Simple View of Reading to consider as well that also inform teachers' reading instruction. To explore some of those, we use McKenna and Stahl's (2009) cognitive model of reading comprehension. In the model, language comprehension is present, but it includes specific components, including vocabulary knowledge, background knowledge, and knowledge of text and sentence structures. A visual of what McKenna and Stahl include in what makes up language comprehension is in Figure 10.1. Next, the cognitive model also includes the decoding/fluency component described in the Simple View, but again it is expanded to help see some components of the process, which include alphabet knowledge, print concepts, phonological awareness, decoding and sight word knowledge, automatic word recognition, and fluency in text reading. Thus, in the cognitive model, the decoding component is conceptualized in more detail that may be helpful to know for teaching practice. Finally, the model includes the pragmatics of reading, such as the purpose of reading and how people use their knowledge of reading strategies to engage in strategic reading. While we accept the model and its components, we feel that it still is not complete. There is a need to consider and include the artful and affective dimensions of reading and learning to read.

A New Model of Reading

We would like to propose a model that blends the art and science of reading, a model we call the Engaged Reading Model. The formula is below.

Fluency + comprehension + motivation = engaged reading

In this model, fluency would include decoding skills, accuracy, automaticity, and prosody. Reading comprehension, rather than the end result, is included here because it is required for engaged reading. We have also added motivation, which is often neglected in models for reading. The motivation component can be increased by teachers who incorporate innovative, authentic, and artful instruction in order to further develop fluent readers who comprehend text proficiently. When combined, fluency, comprehension, and motivation can promote the notion of engaged reading. Guthrie (2001) explains engaged reading as the combination of motivation and thoughtfulness. That is, students care about the processes and outcomes of their reading, and they see the connection of the reading task to something authentic. Teachers artfully arrange reading instruction to help students see a real purpose for reading, which students are intrinsically motivated to pursue.

Prominent Learning Theories in Literacy and Implications for Instructional Development

In this section, we will look specifically at some commonly used theories used to frame or develop potentially effective approaches to reading instruction. We know that theories may not be at the forefront of teachers' minds when writing curriculum, as theories are often seen as a somewhat erroneous addition to courses in educator preparation programs. Honestly, some of us thought that, too. After graduation and certification, we leave the theories behind. Fortunately, in our teaching careers and beyond, we revisited theories of reading to guide our instruction and revolutionize the way we taught our students. In this final chapter, we hope to show that theories can actually provide a practical framework for instructional development.

Social Constructivism

We will start with a commonly cited theory used widely in education. Lev Vygosky is revered as the founder of social constructivism. Social constructivism claims that knowledge is socially situated and that learning can occur through social interaction. With this in mind, Vygotsky (1978) lays out four tenets of this theory: 1) the zone of proximal development (ZPD), 2) semiotic mediation, 3) concept development, and 4) internalization. We will explain each of these, their implications for instruction, and how teachers can use all four tenets to develop research- and theory-based reading instruction.

First, the ZPD essentially represents the range where instruction is maximized. That is, the content or tasks are not too easy and not too difficult – it is challenging and helps move the student forward in their learning. A widely used example of this is found in the use of instructional leveled texts. The instructional level is above a student's independent reading level, a level where students can successfully read texts by themselves, and it is below their frustrational level, which is exactly as it sounds – a level that may frustrate a student. Thus, the instructional level is within the student's ZPD, meaning that it is appropriate for learning and further development of their reading ability.

Semiotic mediation is Vygosky's fancy term for what fundamentally means people learn through dialogue. Thus, teachers want their students to talk and work together. There are many examples in classrooms that use this tenet, including literature circles, buddy reading, think-pair-share, Readers' Theater, and any other activity that requires students to work in partners or collaborative groups. Shotter (1993) claimed that this interaction through dialogue can initiate cognitive restructuring, which can lead to concept development – the third tenet. The experiences and thoughts of others interact with a student's own knowledge and experience to learn a new concept or understand a concept through a new perspective or with increased sophistication. Words from Lindfors (1987) sum this tenet up nicely: "Verbal interaction serves as an important function by getting us to new ideas or observations, taking us beyond the limits of our experience" (p. 273).

Finally, the student internalizes the socially constructed knowledge. Of course, students do not internalize the knowledge created through social interaction verbatim; instead, they internalize a coherent understanding that makes sense to them. While the internalization may not resemble the individual understandings of all of those involved in the interaction, the social interaction plays a major role in the construction of their private knowledge. In summary, we give students an appropriately challenging task, encourage dialogue and the respectful exchange of ideas, and allow students to reflect on their newly developed concepts and internalize a coherent understanding of the experience as new private knowledge.

Existing Classroom Practices

Now, here are a couple existing classroom practices that are clearly based on a social constructivist framework to get a better idea of how teachers can use theory to inform their reading instruction. Particular approaches to literature circles follow all four of Vygostky's tenets. In addition, research suggests that it is an effective and authentic approach to literacy learning (McElvain, 2010). First, the teacher chooses texts for the students based on interest and readability (ZPD). Next, students read sections or chapters of the book to prepare for a literature circle discussion. At that point, students who are reading the same text meet in a group to discuss (semiotic mediation). Through the discussion, students are encouraged to ask questions and seek clarification of aspects of the text to gain a better understanding (concept development). Finally, teachers allow a time of reflection where students can think about what they read combined with what they learned from the discussion and write their final thoughts about the text in a reading journal (internalization). In addition, literature circles are a good example of an activity where engaged reading is the ultimate goal.

Literature circles are also considered artful because it is an authentic activity. People attend book clubs in the real world, an activity begun in the United States in 1878 (Chautauqua Literacy and Scientific Circle, n.d.). At those clubs, you would not have seen members answering multiple-choice questions or quizzing each other; rather, people would have been talking about the book. In literature circles, people talk about what they liked, what they did not like, the deeper meaning, or even how the lessons learned can be used in their own lives. The next activity, jigsaw, is an authentic approach because in the real world, we often rely on experts.

The jigsaw strategy is another good example of social constructivism in the classroom (Slavin, 1995). It is a widely used strategy for which there is research support (Maring, Furman, & Blum-Anderson, 1985). In this strategy, the primary goal is to learn an entirely new concept, which should and can be challenging (ZPD). The concept is then divided into components. For example, the concept we are discussing here is social constructivism, and there are four tenets or components. To begin, students are assigned a concept group, and then each of the members is assigned a component. Next, the groups shift and students with the same assigned component meet together. For example, everyone assigned ZPD would then meet as a group. In that group, their goal is to become experts on their component. They might read articles, search the Internet, tap their own knowledge, and discuss their learning (semiotic mediation). The goal of the discussion is to arrive at a somewhat coherent understanding of the component and prepare to teach their concept group about their component. Once sufficiently prepared, the members leave their component groups and rejoin the concept group, where they will take turns teaching each component to develop an understanding of the entire concept (concept development). After each shares, and through more semiotic mediation and concept development, students in each group write about or demonstrate what they have learned (internalization).

Indeed, as we become more adept at our teaching, we begin to formulate our own theories that emerge not only from the theories we have learned in the past but also from our own practice and what we have experienced and learned through our practice as teachers and how students have responded to that practice.

Developing a New Classroom Practice

We are now about to develop a new classroom practice that is both theoretically rooted in social constructivism as well as based on empirical research in reading. At the moment of this writing, there is no clear idea in mind. This section will be written in the first person from the author's perspective. The thinking and development of whatever happens to follow truly begins now.

I (Chase) just had an aha moment. I was thinking about social constructivism, common curricular units taught in elementary grade levels, and research on word recognition, vocabulary, reading comprehension, and fluency. All of these thoughts mixed in my head, and something wonderful emerged. I call this strategy "Finding Loot with Poetry." Trust me, you heard it here first.

First, I will give you a quick overview of what I have come up with, and then I will talk you through the specifics of the theories and research combined with my thought processes.

1. The teacher steals something small from one of the students while they are at specials, lunch, or out of the classroom.

2. The teacher hides the stolen object on the playground, outside elsewhere, or in the classroom.

3. The teacher writes or selects an existing poem that will serve as a clue about the object's location.

4. Students are assigned small groups or partners.

5. The teacher passes out the poem to each group.

6. The teacher reads the poem to the students while they follow along.

7. The groups then read the poem chorally.

8. Each student reads their copy of the poem to themselves while thinking carefully about the meaning.

9. For about five to ten minutes, the groups discuss the meaning of the poem, revisiting or rereading the text as necessary. Students also discuss how the meaning might relate to the location of the stolen object.

10. After the time is up, students are allowed to physically seek the object in the location the groups agreed upon.

11. When students find the object, it is returned to the student.

12. Individually, students recall their group's discussion of the various interpretations of the poem and write down the meaning of the poem and their reasoning behind their interpretation.

So, now I cover some theory and research that inspired the newly developed "Finding Loot with Poetry." I thought first about the social constructivist framework. In order to ensure that there was some interaction, I decided that students would be organized into groups. To allow for semiotic mediation, I required a discussion about the meaning of the text and how that meaning relates to the location of the object. Discovering the concept of the intended meaning should be the primary purpose of the discussion, hence the inclusion of concept development as a result of the dialogue. Finally, I required students to write down their internalized interpretation.

I wanted to ensure that we had some challenging material, so I had to come up with a grade level. I settled on first or second grade. I also thought about typical curricular units, and I know that poetry comes up often, and thus I settled on using poetry as the text. I looked through several websites with existing children's poetry and found some that could be useful for this activity. I found poems about sickness (the nurse's office) and poems about working out (the gym), and these were easily found by searching for "poems about _____" on the Internet. However, in the end, I wrote my own:

I dare not go up it

The watchers will frown

I politely go down

With a yee and a wee

And deetle dattle dee

The ground I meet

Never forget

It's a one-way street.

The next step involves a research-based approach to building reading fluency, a component in the Engaged Reading Model. The teacher first reads the poem aloud to model accurate word reading, pacing, and expression (Farrell, 1966). The students then engage in a choral reading of the text (Paige, 2011). Then, the students read their own copy of the poem and think carefully about the meaning of the poem. This will prepare them for their group discussion, which is similar to a literature circle discussion, but it has a more focused purpose – finding the meaning of the poem in order to locate the stolen object. To address the comprehension component, research (Clark, 2009; Young & Mohr, 2018) suggests that discussing and reflecting on texts with peers in small groups can improve students' understanding of a text. As Edmund Burke once said, "Reading without reflecting is like eating without digesting." This small-group or partner discussion is a form of semiotic mediation which leads to concept development and eventually internalization. But first, the class gets some physical activity as they search for the object, which, in this case, would be on the slide on the playground. After the great recovery of the object, students internalize their learning in the last step that requires them to write down the meaning and provide a rationale for their interpretation of the poem.

So, in the end, I am fairly pleased with how I used social constructivist theory as well as the Engaged Reading Model to construct a potentially engaging and effective approach to reading instruction. In an artful weave of instruction, students have developed their fluency and comprehension and were motivated to read in order to find the stolen object, resulting in engaged reading. While analyzing poetry is not new to classrooms, the approach was designed into a new form – a work of art, indeed. Naturally, I had my past students in mind and used my teacher judgment to decide what might engage my students into the reading process. Honestly, it really did not even take that long (the idea – not the writing), and truly I would have never come up with "Finding Loot with Poetry" had I not considered the theory, research, and components of the Engaged Reading Model that could be creatively and effectively arranged into something new and exciting.

Cognitive Learning Theory

Cognitive learning theory is a branch of constructivism that is concerned how the mind works and primarily focuses on processes of learning and not products of learning. Although this is a broadly based theory, we will focus mainly on instruction that encourages critical thinking and empha-sizes mental processes over completing assignments. We believe that read-ing instruction in this realm should stimulate deeper thought and provide students opportunities to hypothesize, theorize, and engage in discovery. We will first cover two examples of existing practices that use cognitive learning theory as a foundation. Then, similar to the previous section, a new artful approach will be developed using theory and existing research.

Existing Classroom Practices

The concept attainment strategy is a good example of an approach deeply rooted in cognitive learning theory. It is a deductive teaching and learn-ing style that helps students use particular examples in order to generate their own understanding of a concept. The concept attainment strategy is a highly effective strategy used to teach for understanding. The strategy requires students to reason, and teachers spark curiosity by essentially con-fusing students to the point where they are able to organize their thoughts until they are able to describe the critical attributes of a concept and ana-lyze the concept in different contexts (Silver, Hanson, Strong, & Schwartz, 2003).

The steps are relatively clear:

1. Identify a concept.

2. Generate examples and nonexamples.

3. Draw two (or more) columns and label them as A and B (and so on).

4. Provide an example and a nonexample in the two columns.

5. Ask students to hypothesize how the example and nonexample are different and describe the characteristics of each.

6. The teacher then provides another example and nonexample.

7. Students think about how the examples and nonexamples are dif-ferent as well as what makes those in the same column similar.

8. The teacher continues to add examples while students make and revise their hypotheses and continue to describe the characteris-tics of each column of examples.

For example, the concept attainment strategy has been used to determine the difference between a main idea and details in a text. The examples will be derived from *Skippyjon Jones* by Judy Schachner. Here is how this would play out in the classroom. The teacher adds one example of a main idea and one nonexample, which happen to simply be details.

A	B
Skippyjon Jones is a Siamese cat that wants to be a Chihuahua.	Skippyjon Jones takes a bath in Mrs. Doohiggy's birdbath.

At this point, the teacher asks the students to describe the differences. The teacher writes down all of their observations. In this case, students might notice that one sentence is longer than the other, which may not be too helpful in the long run. The teacher then adds one more row.

A	B
Skippyjon Jones is a Siamese cat that wants to be a Chihuahua.	Skippyjon Jones takes a bath in Mrs. Doohiggy's birdbath.
Skippyjon Jones has a wild imagination and goes on adventures.	Skippyjon Jones is sent to his room.

Well, unfortunately for the students, the length of the sentence no longer matters, so they have to revise their hypotheses regarding the differences. A student might now say that column A has statements that were not found directly in the text, while column B has information they read in the text. Students can now also analyze similarities of the statements found in the same columns.

A	B
Skippyjon Jones is a Siamese cat that wants to be a Chihuahua.	Skippyjon Jones takes a bath in Mrs. Doohiggy's birdbath.
Skippyjon Jones has a wild imagination and goes on adventures.	Skippyjon Jones is sent to his room.
Skippyjon Jones imagines he is a great sword fighter and is a hero and always saves the day.	Skippyjon Jones is sent to bed by his mother.

The teacher presents another row and prompts the students with questions such as, "Why are these statements in column A? Why are these in column B? What makes them different? How are the statements in column A alike? What about column B?" Students will provide various answers that will help them first understand the premises, particulars, and details that make up what we understand as the main idea.

In the end, we name the columns. Column A is the main idea of the story one might infer throughout the text. The nonexamples are simply details within the text. Students will be required to determine the critical attributes of the examples, or the main idea. They should understand that these attributes include an overall explanation of the story, the point the author is making about the topic, the most important concept of the story, the central thought of the text, or what the story is mostly about. At this point, students should be able to generate their own examples of the main idea and express a coherent definition of main idea.

Certainly, this could be considered an artful approach to learning a key concept in reading comprehension. Teachers often introduce the concept of main idea and then attempt to explain what it means, which is considered inductive. Of course, it makes sense when you are required to teach the concept of main idea to do just that: "Okay, students, we are going to learn about the main idea of the story. Main idea is . . ." However, artful teachers think carefully about whether the students in their classrooms learn best in this way. If not, the teacher judgment kicks in, and you consider what you know about the students. If they seem to light up, interact, or engage more when they participate in the construction of learning, you might use a deductive approach similar to the concept attainment strategy.

The Mystery Strategy is another approach that aligns nicely with cognitive learning theory. It is a high-interest activity that puts the learner in a scenario where they work with their own abilities, and that of their peers, to draw conclusions about a discrepancy delivered by the teacher. There are four phases that students pass through in this strategy. The first step is to encounter a problem and conjure a hypothesis. Next, they examine clues and create order, or sort the clues. After thorough examination, students refine and test their hypothesis according to the data. Finally, students draw a conclusion and present their findings based on their interpretation of the evidence.

The teacher's role is significant in formulating the mystery. There are five steps that must be completed before the mystery can be brought to the students. The first task of the teacher is to create a problem. For this example, the origin of the moon will be discussed. In order to hook the students, a list of words will be read aloud. Students will be encouraged to make connections, visual images, and predictions based on the words read; the teacher reads *earth, moon, magma, asteroids, planets, energy, billions of years, debris, impact,* and *birth.*

Each student will receive clues (Appendix A) that will help them make connections, examine cause and effect relationships, and help support their hypotheses. The teacher then establishes a scenario. For example, the teacher might tell students that the origin of the moon has been debated by scientists all over the world, which is true. Now, the scientists have asked for the students to help in the research and develop theories around the origin of the moon, which is not true. They then begin using the clues, sorting them if necessary, and refining their hypothesis as needed.

Both the concept attainment and mystery strategies align closely to cognitivism, as the approaches are focused more on mental processing rather than a final product. Deciding what approach to take, and how to arrange it to best meet the needs of your students, is what underlies artful teaching. You should also be thinking about how you might use the concepts discussed thus far and how you might design your own artful approaches to reading instruction.

Developing a New Classroom Practice

As I (Chase) begin to think about developing a new strategy this time, I start with an objective and intended grade level. Let's focus on older elementary grades and try a new spin on learning how to infer character motivations with a real-world example. Seriously, I just sat back in my chair, thought for about three minutes, and here we go. I call this one "What Makes a Teacher?"

First, here is a brief overview of the approach and then I will spend time explaining the theoretical and research connections.

1. The teacher poses the following question to the students: "What are the primary reasons people choose to become teachers?"

171

2. The teacher explains that the students will be conducting research online to answer this question.

3. The teacher facilitates the brainstorming of possible search terms or phrases, such as *diary of a teacher, why I became a teacher, why I love teaching,* or any other potentially helpful phrases the students come up with.

4. Yes, the students are about to engage in qualitative research to identify common themes in teacher posts, blogs, diaries, or websites that describe why people decide to become teachers.

a. I just googled qualitative research with kids and there was nothing about what I am proposing here. It was all about conducting qualitative research with child participants, so I am pretty excited about this idea.

5. Students then spend time searching the Internet and identifying helpful sources.

6. When reading the sources, students take notes and write down every time they come across statements relevant to the question at hand.

7. After reading at least ten sources, the students then look for common themes.

8. The students write down the themes and provide evidence of why they concluded that those themes were more dominant.

The process of data collection and analysis is certainly the bulk of the work in "What Makes a Teacher?" The process is always emphasized in qualitative research, as it is always explained in great detail. Thus, it is clear the cognitivists would be satisfied with this approach. Also, looking for emergent themes in data is the epitome of deductive learning. Making sense of tiny pieces and putting them together to draw conclusions is a worthy mental exercise, and the concept fits nicely with the Engaged Reading Model.

Next, what is the research that supports this approach? First, inquiry-based reading instruction in online environments is necessary for the world we live in (Hoch, McCarty, Gurvitz, & Sitkoski, 2019). In addition, setting a purpose for reading is another research-based way to promote engagement and closer readings of texts (Boardman, Buckley, Lasser, Klingner, & Annamma, 2015). In the "What Makes a Teacher?" activity, students have one overarching goal, which is to answer the primary question. There are also several small goals, including using effective search terms, identifying helpful sources, reading carefully, and taking notes that will be useful to analyze. Thus, there are several purposes, and setting multiple purposes can also increase engagement (Nolen, 2001). In the end, the same type of thinking practiced in "What Makes a Teacher?" can also be used to understand the motivations of fictional characters. Making this connection by learning in a real-world example may help students better understand the concept of inferring character motivations.

What makes this artful instruction? It is the combination of creativity and authenticity. Indeed, it is fun to think about engaging elementary students in qualitative research such as this. It allows students plenty of choice in the sources they use and what they feel is most important in each. Taking those pieces of important details and thinking critically about how they are related to construct themes requires plenty of creativity. Creativity is also necessary in the presentation of those themes. The activity is also authentic because it is real. The investigation has likely been done by educational researchers because it is important know. Thus, we have created something that engages reading and thinking to understand something that truly matters.

Now, I know what you are thinking. Does it have to be a teacher? Absolutely not. It can be anything and should be something of interest to your students. And that thinking means you are well on your way to developing some artful, innovative, and effective approaches to reading instruction.

Final Thoughts

This book has really been about empowering you as teachers – as scientists as well as artists. You have the power and the knowledge to combine scientific theory and research and artfully arrange and create instruction that is effective, engaging, and authentic and that meets the needs of your students. We hope you enjoyed this experience.

References

Boardman, A., Buckley, P., Lasser, C., Klingner, J., & Annamma, S. (2015). The efficacy of collaborative strategic reading in middle school science and social studies classes. *Reading & Writing, 28*(9), 1257–1283.

Chautauqua Literacy and Scientific Circle. (n.d.). Retrieved from https://chq.org/phocadownload/LiteraryArts/CLSCBookList.pdf

Clark, K. F. (2009). The nature and influence of comprehension strategy use during peer-led literature discussions: An analysis of intermediate grade students' practice. *Literacy Research and Instruction, 48*(2), 95–119.

Farrell, E. (1966). Listen, my children, and you shall read . . . *English Journal, 55,* 39–45.

Gough, P. B., & Tunmer, W. E. (1986). Decoding, reading, and reading disability. *Remedial and Special Education, 7,* 6–10.

Guthrie, J. T. (2001). Contexts for engagement and motivation in reading. *Reading Online, 4*(8). International Reading Association: Washington DC.

Hoch, M. L., McCarty, R., Gurvitz, D., & Sitkoski, I. (2019). Five key principles: Guided inquiry with multimodal text sets. *Reading Teacher, 72*(6), 701–710.

LaBerge, D., & Samuels, J. (1974). Towards a theory of automatic information processing in reading. *Cognitive Psychology, 6,* 293–323.

Lindfors, J. (1987). *Children's language and learning.* Boston: Prentice-Hall.

Maring, G. H., Furman, G. C., & Blum-Anderson, J. (1985). Five cooperative learning strategies for mainstreamed youngsters in content area classrooms. *Reading Teacher, 39*(3), 310–313.

McElvain, C. M. (2010). Transactional literature circles and the reading comprehension of English learners in the mainstream classroom. *Journal of Research in Reading, 33*(2), 178–205. doi:10.1111/j.1467-9817.2009.01403.x

McKenna, M. C., & Stahl, K. A. (2009). *Assessment for reading instruction* (2nd ed.). New York: Guilford Press.

Nolen, S. B. (2001). Constructing literacy in the kindergarten: Task structure, collaboration, and motivation. *Cognition and Instruction, 19*(1), 95–142.

Paige, D. (2011). "That sounded good!": Using whole-class choral reading to improve fluency. *The Reading Teacher, 64*(6), 435–438.

Silver, H. F., Hanson, J. R., Strong, R. W., & Schwartz, P. B. (2003). *Teaching styles & strategies.* Ho-Ho-Kus, NJ: The Thoughtful Education Press.

Slavin, R. E. (1995). *Cooperative learning: Theory, research, and practice* (2nd ed.). Boston: Allyn & Bacon.

Shotter, J. (1993). Vygotsky: The social negotiation of semiotic mediation. *New Ideas in Psychology, 11*(1), 61–75. doi:10.1016/0732-118X(93)90020-E

Vygotsky, L. S. (1978). *Mind in society: The development of higher psychological processes.* Cambridge, MA: Harvard University Press.

Young, C., & Mohr, K. (2018). Exploring factors that influence quality literature circles. *Literacy Research and Instruction, 57*(1), 44–58.

Appendix A

Clue
> The Earth has a large iron core, but the moon does not.

Clue
> The Earth has no iron in the crust because it has all drained to the core.

Clue
> Objects often collide in space.

Clue
> When objects collide, debris floats in space.

Clue
> Earth has a density of 5.5 g/cc, but the moon has a density of only 3.3 g/cc. The reason is the same: the moon lacks iron.

Clue
> The moon has exactly the same oxygen isotope composition as the Earth, whereas Mars rocks and meteorites from other parts of the solar system have different oxygen isotope compositions.

Clue
> A small planet the size of Mars struck the Earth just after the formation of the solar system, ejecting large volumes of heated material from the outer layers of both objects.

Clue

Mercury and Venus have no moons at all.

Clue

Much of Earth's crust folds under and recycles every 150 million years or so.

Clue

The mineral composition of moon rocks – including elements such as iron, silicon, magnesium, and manganese – resembles that of Earth rocks.

Clue

The moon is moving away from Earth by more than an inch a year. The moon was much closer to Earth when it formed more than four billion years ago. Today it's about 240,000 miles away. Originally the distance might have been only 16,000 miles. It would have loomed 15 times larger in the sky had anyone been around to see it.

Clue

The lunar samples had been found to contain a large proportion of low-density minerals, and the only plausible explanation anyone had proposed was that the moon's surface had once been almost entirely molten.

Clue

When large objects collide, it produces heat. If two objects collided like Earth and a bit smaller planet, it would create temperatures up to 18,000 degrees.

Clue

The only way to get a magmatic ocean is to assemble the moon very rapidly, and the only way to do that is to have debris in Earth's orbit.

Index

Note: Page numbers in *italics* indicate a figure and page numbers in **bold** indicate a table on the corresponding page.

Made in the USA
Columbia, SC
25 September 2022

67902308R00104